Crystal's Curiosity Cabinet

Crystal's Curiosity Cabinet

An English Language Miscellany

David Crystal

Chambers

First published in Great Britain by Chambers in 2025
An imprint of John Murray Press

1

A CIP catalogue record for this title is available from the British Library

Hardback ISBN 978 1 39982 389 0
ebook ISBN 9 781 39982 390 6

Typeset by KnowledgeWorks Global Ltd.

Printed and bound in Great Britain by Clays Ltd, Elcograf S.p.A.

John Murray Press policy is to use papers that are natural, renewable and recyclable products and made from wood grown in sustainable forests. The logging and manufacturing processes are expected to conform to the environmental regulations of the country of origin.

John Murray Press
Carmelite House
50 Victoria Embankment
London EC4Y 0DZ

Chambers
Hachette Book Group
123 South Broad Street
Ste 2750
Philadelphia, PA 19109, USA

www.chambers.co.uk

John Murray Press, part of Hodder & Stoughton Limited
An Hachette UK company

The authorized representative in the EEA is Hachette Ireland, 8 Castlecourt Centre, Dublin 15, D15 XTP3, Ireland (email: info@hbgi.ie)

Contents

Preface

Anyone with an interest in language is likely to be an observer and collector of curiosities, and often a contributor. And when the interest is lifelong, the collection can become quite large. I've been a collector as long as I can remember. Many of the findings I've been able to use in various books, but there are always items that don't fit into anything, and remain gathering dust in a bottom drawer – or, these days, in a computer file labelled 'miscellaneous'. I've brought the English-language ones out of retirement for this book.

The pieces were accumulated serendipitously, encountered through listening, reading, and lecturing in local, national, and global situations, and the randomness is reflected here. Several are favourite extracts from books and magazines. Some are selections from dictionaries and other reference works, chosen to capture their general character. The personal contributions always came out of reactions to radio programmes, conference talks, or blog posts.

The topics are wide-ranging and reflect many of the language issues that loom large in the popular mind, such as accents, dialects etymology, proverbs, place names, punctuation, everyday usage, and language change. Recurrent themes are global as well as national, historical as well as present-day. Another perspective is literary, with Shakespeare, Dickens, and Swift accompanied by neglected personalities such as Tom Brown and writers from the pages of *Punch* magazine.

The desire to be playful with language motivates many of the pieces, and in these pages I send a nostalgic wave to the ludic enthusiasts of the 20th century, such as Ross Eckler, Willard Espy, and Dmitri Borgmann. I continue this theme into the 21st century, illustrating how people like to outdo each other in inventiveness, even in situations where language play might seem a distant prospect, such as during a pandemic.

The collection follows in the tradition of Elizabethan commonplace books and Victorian cabinets of curiosities. Encountering linguistic creativity, in its many forms, has been an endless source of fascination, and I hope that delight will transfer to readers of this anthology.

Baptism?

THIS is a word that's always been used in relation to people, so I was surprised to find it being applied to an object.

To mark the 40th anniversary of the Hvězda Cinema in the small Czech town of Uherské Hradiště, the organisers had published an illustrated memorial book to mark the occasion. Along with the festival director and one of the sponsors, I was invited to be a godfather for the book. It was to be 'baptised'. We stood at the front of the cinema while a copy of the book was brought on, resting on a tray. On top of the book were three glasses of white wine. After a few words from the director, we each took up a glass and then ... solemnly poured it over the book. (The soaked book was greatly valued and would raise a goodly sum at auction.)

I had not come across this tradition anywhere else, but I introduced it to Wales in 2012, when the first collection of writings by Anglesey authors, *Môntage*, was launched at the town hall in Llangefni – but using red wine this time. (*Môntage* puns on the Welsh name for the Isle of Anglesey, Ynys Môn.)

I am by no means the first to be a book's godfather. In the preface to the long narrative poem *Venus and Adonis* (1593), we read that Shakespeare dedicated the work to Henry Wriothesley, 3rd Earl of Southampton (1573–1624), and calls him its godfather. I'd like to think that a cup of sack was poured over a copy.

So, I pour an imaginary glass of wine over this entry, to launch my *Miscellany*.

A Victorian univocalic – *A*

ONE of the word-games the Victorians liked to play was to construct poems in which all the words contained the same vowel – *univocalics*. Here's an example from 1875, using the letter *A*. It's entitled 'The Russo-Turkish War'. The author is not known.

Wars harm all ranks, all arts, all crafts appall:
At Mars' harsh blast, arch, rampart, altar, fall!
Ah! hard as adamant, a braggart Czar
Arms vassal swarms, and fans a fatal war!
Rampant at that bad call, a Vandal band
Harass, and harm, and ransack Wallach-land.
A Tartar phalanx Balkan's scarp hath past,
And Allah's standard falls, alas! at last.

For the other **univocalics**, see pp. 38, 80, 120, 171.

Collecting collectives – 1

A collective noun is a word that describes a group of things, such as *a herd of cows*, *a flock of sheep*, or *a gaggle of geese*. This has prompted innumerable games and competitions where the aim is to find a humorous collective for a concept. Some of them date from the Middle Ages. These selections illustrate the creative madness that goes on today. Beware: the genre is contagious, and few can read these entries without wanting to do better!

a barrel of guns
a battery of electric cars
a block of trolls
a blush of prize-winners
a body of undertakers
a bond of secret agents
(at least, in Britain)
a bout of boxers
a brace of dentists
a brightness of prodigies
a bungle of DIY enthusiasts
a burst of pipes
a chuckle of comedians

More **collectives** on pp. 32, 66, 133, 181.

Equivocating

ANOTHER Victorian game, author unknown. This one is an extract from a love letter, hidden within a complete text which the lady's objecting father might read. The lover reads only the alternate lines, asterisked here.

To Miss M–

*The great love I have hitherto expressed for you
is false and I find my indifference towards you
*increases daily. The more I see of you, the more
you appear in my eyes an object of contempt.
*I feel myself every way disposed and determined
to hate you. Believe me, I never had an intention
*to offer you my hand. Our last conversation has
left a tedious insipidity, which has by no means
*given me the most exalted view of your character.
Your temper would make me extremely unhappy
*and were we united, I should experience nothing but
the hatred of my parents added to the anything but
*pleasure in living with you. I have indeed a heart
to bestow, but I do not wish you to imagine it
*at your service. I could not give it to anyone more
inconsistent and capricious than yourself, and less
*capable to do honour to my choice and to my family.
Yes, Miss, I hope you will be persuaded that
*I speak sincerely, and you will do me a favor
to avoid me. I shall excuse you taking the trouble

*to answer this. Your letters are always full of
impertinence, and you have not a shadow of
*wit and good sense. Adieu! Adieu! believe me
so averse to you, that it is impossible for me ever
*to be your most affectionate friend and humble
servant.

For another **equivocation**, see p. 91.

Dickens' voice portraits - 1

In *Our Mutual Friend* (1865), of Bradley Headstone:

> Grinding his words slowly out, as though they came from a rusty mill.

More **voice portraits** on pp. 48, 84, 147, 204.

There's a catch(phrase)

JOSEPH Heller's novel *Catch-22* (1961) is one of the few novel titles to have given a word to the English language as a whole: we routinely talk of a 'catch-22 situation'. Usually, artistic titles reflect what is already in a language (e.g. *Great Expectations*) rather than contribute something new to it. In fact, Heller's original name for the book was *Catch-18*, but just before publication it was noticed that another novel with a similar title was due out at the same time: Leon Uris's *Mila 18*. So the publisher added four to the name to avoid any confusion. It was an inspired phonaesthetic choice. To see this, imagine knocking on a door with the rhythm of *Catch-22* and compare it with a knock which has the rhythm of *Catch-18*. The extra syllable adds a noticeable pace and urgency. I wonder whether the original title, with its more leisurely auditory connotation, would ever have entered the language?

The Wright story

OF all the characters that lie behind many of the entries in this book, none to my mind beats the story of Joseph Wright (1855–1930), whose masterwork was the six-volume *English Dialect Dictionary*, published between 1898 and 1905, which he financed himself. It took him 23 years to collect all the material – around 117,500 senses of words, taken from over 3,000 dialect glossaries, works containing dialect words, and the contributions of over 600 voluntary readers and correspondents.

He was born in Thackley, a village in West Yorkshire. When he was six, he got a job driving a donkey cart, carrying tools belonging to local stoneworkers. A year later he was working half a day in a cotton mill, replacing full bobbins on the hundreds of spinning machines by empty ones. The other half day was spent in the local primary school – though this, he later said, taught him very little. He learned to read and write using the Bible and Bunyan's *Pilgrim's Progress*, and was self-educated through a weekly purchase of Cassell's *Popular Educator*.

Two or three evenings each week he went to a local night-school, where he began to learn French and German. By the time he was 20, he'd taught himself Latin and shorthand. He became a schoolteacher and saved enough to train as a philologist at Heidelberg University, before taking up a post at Oxford in 1888. There's no other linguistic story quite as dramatic as the one in which an illiterate quarry-boy and millworker becomes a professor of comparative philology at Oxford University.

For examples of **dialect words** from Wright's dictionary, see pp. 49, 81, 134, 188.

Comic alphabets – 1

ONE of the many comic alphabets aimed at children, especially popular during the 19th century. The author is unknown.

A was an apple-pie

B bit it
C cut it
D dealt it
E eat it
F fought for it
G got it
H had it
I inspected it
J joined for it
K kept it
L longed for it
M mourned for it
N nodded at it
O opened it
P peeped in it
Q quartered it
R ran for it
S stole it
T took it
U upset it
V viewed it
W wanted it

X, Y, Z and Ampersand
All wish'd for a piece in hand.

For more **comic alphabets**, see pp. 64, 135, 179, 202.

How much, did you say? – 1

A series of articles in *Around the Globe* (2012), the magazine of Shakespeare's Globe, explored the value of references to money in Elizabethan England, many of which are obscure today. A *crown* is a case in point.

In Act 3 of *All's Well That Ends Well*, Helena devises a cunning plan to ignite the affections of her alienated husband, Bertram, for which she needs the help of her new acquaintances, a widow and her daughter (who Bertram fancies). The widow is naturally suspicious, but Helena persuades her:

> You see it lawful then. It is no more
> But that your daughter, ere she seems as won,
> Desires this ring; appoints him an encounter;
> In fine, delivers me to fill the time,
> Herself most chastely absent. After,
> To marry her I'll add three thousand crowns
> To what is passed already.
>
> WIDOW: I have yielded.

How should the actors say the last two lines? It's not enough for Helena to speak the financial inducement in a routinely cajoling tone of voice, and for the Widow to reply in the tone of 'Oh well, then, all right', for 3,000 crowns was a lot of money. A crown was a gold coin of varying value in different countries, but in the England of Shakespeare's time it was worth about 5 shillings, a quarter of an old pound. Three thousand crowns was therefore about £750.

According to the website of The National Archives, £1 in 1600 is equivalent to around £100 today. So, Helena was offering the widow about £75,000 in today's money. No wonder she yields so readily. The point is missed unless we get a 'wait for it' pause after 'add' in Helena's offer and a truly amazed ('gulp') reaction. And it illustrates just how much Helena wants her husband back.

For more **How much ...?**, see pp. 42, 92, 144, 205.

Proverbial wisdom - 1

A translation of proverbs from around the world, from my *As They Say in Zanzibar* (2006).

A proverb places the words in one's mouth. [Switzerland]
'Tis a good word that can better a good silence. [Netherlands]
Good words make us laugh; good deeds make us silent. [France]
Small cares make many words; great ones are mute. [Germany]
Words do not make flour. [Italy]
A kind word warms for three winters. [China]
A true word is not beautiful and a beautiful word is not true. [Japan]
Words will pay for most things. [Spain]
A good word never broke a tooth. [Ireland]
Who does not understand half a word will not be wiser for a whole word. [Finland]

And from England:

Actions speak louder than words.
Many a true word is spoke in jest.

For more **proverbial wisdom**, see pp. 51, 104, 156, 182.

Excuse me?

STARTING a conversation with someone at a party is often the hardest part. So, in 1996, a group of researchers at the Media Laboratory of the Massachusetts Institute of Technology came up with the idea of *Groupware* – a lapel badge that lights up when you meet someone with similar interests. When people arrive at the party, they answer a small set of questions and their answers are coded onto the badges. The badge has five small lights which can flash either red or green. When two wearers meet, their badges communicate by infrared beams and swap data about their owners. The more alike the interests, the more the green lights show, and vice versa. Either display, evidently, could start a good conversation.

A glorious lipogram

A lipogram, a word of Greek origin, refers to a text that 'leaves out a letter'. Anyone wishing to explore the genre in English will find the greatest challenge in *e*, which occurs far more frequently than any other letter, and disallows such important words as *the*, past tense forms ending in *-ed*, and much more. Ernest Vincent Wright (1872–1939), from Los Angeles, achieved lasting fame in the world of English language playfulness by publishing in 1939 a 50,000-word *e*-less novel, *Gadsby*. To make sure no instances inadvertently slipped in, he tied down the *e*-bar on his typewriter. The result has been praised for its naturalistic descriptions and dialogue. Here's an example from the middle of the story:

> As Gadsby stood, on a chilly fall day, in front of that
> big glass building which was built for a city florist,
> admiring a charming display of blossoming plants,
> a small girl, still in Grammar School, said, shyly:-
>
> 'Hulloa.'
> 'Hulloa, you. School out?'
> 'On Saturdays, school is always out.'
> 'That's so; it *is* Saturday, isn't it? Going in?'
> '*In!!* My, no! *I* can't go into that fairyland.'
> 'No? Why not, pray?'

'Aw, I dunno; but nobody has took kids -'
'Took? Took? Say, young lady, you must study your grammar book.'

Gadsby was reprinted by the American independent publisher Ramble House in 2004 and has been through several editions.

Wellerisms

A Wellerism typically has three parts: a statement of some kind, usually idiomatic or proverbial; a speaker identification; and an incongruous situation or recipient that adds a humorous twist. The name comes from Charles Dickens' character Sam Weller and his father, though the genre is much older, and has been traced back to classical antiquity. Here's an example from *The Pickwick Papers* (1837):

> 'How are you, ma'am?' said Mr Weller. 'Wery glad to see you, indeed, and hope our acquaintance may be a long 'un, as the gen'l'm'n said to the fi' pun' note.'

Examples from the 19th century

'I'll try another bit,' as the jockey said when his horse ran away with him.
'Yours is a very hard case,' as the fox said to the oyster.
'I'll let you know when I come back again,' as the rheumatism said to the leg.
'Won't suit me at all,' as the man said to the tailor who refused him credit.
'So I'm told,' as the church bell remarked when it heard of the villager's death.

Examples from the 20th century

> 'A little behind in my work,' said the butcher as he backed into the meat grinder.
> 'I beg your pardon!' sang the convict, as the governor passed down the corridor.
> 'I got the point,' said the man as he brushed the wasp off his neck.
> 'We'll have to rehearse that,' said the undertaker, as the coffin fell out of the car.
> 'Hell, yes!' murmured the devil, picking up the phone receiver.

The genre continued into the 20th century, with many adaptations, such as the suggestive '... as the actress said to the bishop' used by detective fiction writer Leslie Charteris, and the Tom Swifties (p. 34) that parodied the style of young adult adventure books.

Mosaics

THE *cento* was another popular Victorian pastime – the word is from Latin, where it meant a patchwork garment – also called *mosaic* or *collage* verse. The aim is to compose a poem where each line comes from the work of another poet or poets, put together in a new way. Here are the first two stanzas from a 40-line creation that appeared in *The People's Friend* in May 1871. The numbers identify the authors.

1. A glorious devil, large in heart and brain,
2. Doomed for a certain term to walk the night,
3. The world forsaking with a calm disdain,
4. Majestic rises on the astonished sight.
5. Type of the wise who soar, but never roam,
6. Mark how it mounts to man's imperial race!
7. High is its perch, but humble is his home,
8. Fast anchored in the deep abyss of space.

1. Alfred, Lord Tennyson 2. William Shakespeare 3. James Thomson
4. J Taite 5. William Wordsworth 6. Alexander Pope
7. James Grahame 8. William Cowper

Global English

THE global use of English provides a further perspective to the story of variation and change, which is one of the themes of this miscellany. Every country that has adopted English, at some point in its history, has adapted it to express its unique culture and setting, and thereby added another dimension to the expressive richness of the language as a whole. The scale of the adaptation is often not appreciated. Even in a small country, such as the Republic of Trinidad and Tobago in the Caribbean, there is a huge local vocabulary, faithfully recorded by Lise Winer in her massive *Dictionary of the English/Creole of Trinidad & Tobago* (2009) – comprising over 12,000 entries of words and idioms that are unique to those islands. Its opening entry contains these examples of proverbial wisdom – a plea for life balance:

> Crab no walk – crab no fat – crab walk too much he come a pot.
> (A crab that doesn't walk will not get fat; a crab that walks too much will be caught and put in a pot')
> = A lazy person amounts to nothing; a person who is too busy will be brought to grief.

The second part is supported by a further image:

> Buckit go a well ebery day, wan day e battam go cum ut.
> = If a bucket goes to a well every day, one day its bottom will fall out.

For a further selection of **Trinidad and Tobago expressions**, see p. 52.

archy writes ...

ONE of my favourite characters in the world of language play is archy, the cockroach created by American writer Don Marquis (1878–1937) who types long poems by jumping on the keys of a typewriter, letter by letter. He isn't able to reach the shift key, so everything is in lower case, and there's no punctuation. In one poem he remembers a meeting with a parrot named Pete, who knew Shakespeare, and who reports how dissatisfied the bard was with his theatre life.

i remember one night when
bill and ben jonson and
frankie beaumont
were sopping it up
here I am ben says bill
nothing but a lousy playwright
and with anything like luck
in the breaks I might have been
a fairly decent sonnet writer
I might have been a poet
if I had kept away from the theatre ...

Variations on a theme

WILLIAM Dobson includes this fine example of poetic anagram exploitation in his *Literary Frivolities* (1880), called 'A Telegram Anagrammatized'.

Though but a *late germ*, with a wondrous elation,
Yet like a *great elm* it o'ershadows each station,
Et malgré the office is still a large fee mart,
So joyous the crowd was, you'd thought it a *glee mart*;
But they raged at no news from the nations belligerent,
And I said, *Let'm rage*, since the air is refrigerant.
I then *met large* numbers, whose drink was not sherbet,
Who scarce could look up when their eyes the gas-*glare met*;
So when I had learned from commercial adviser,
That *mere galt* for sand was the great fertiliser,
I bad *Mr Eaglet*, although 'twas ideal,
Get some from the clay-pit, and so *get 'm real* ...

And so it continues, with a further five variations – *elm targe*, *margelet*, *term gale*, *merle gat*, *get lamer* – before the final couplet:

So I made my escape – ne'er an antelope fleeter,
Lest ny verse, like the poet, should limp through
lag metre.

How did Shakespeare pronounce his name?

AMERICAN linguist David Kathman has collated all the spellings of Shakespeare's name during his lifetime that have survived. The most frequent is the one we use today (190 instances), but there are over 20 variations. The interesting ones are those that drop the first *e* – 87 of them – such as *Shakspeare*, *Shackspere*, *Shaxpere*, and *Shexpere*. They suggest that the first syllable had a short vowel, with a quality somewhere between modern *sat* and *set*.

For the second syllable, rhymes such as *spear* and *there* (in *Venus and Adonis*) point to a vowel quality that must have been more like present-day *spare*, rather than *speer*. Also, being an unstressed syllable, it would have been shorter, as suggested by such spellings as *Shaksper* and *Shaksberd*. And *r*, after a vowel, was always pronounced in those days.

So the evidence points to a pronunciation something like 'Shekspere' or 'Shaksper'.

Verbatim

AMERICAN lexicographer Laurence Urdang (1927–2008) founded *Verbatim* in 1974, 'conceived as an informal, inexpensive periodical for the layman to serve his interests'. It appeared four times a year and grew from its first issue – a thin six-page newsletter – to a chunky 32-pager. Larry edited it until 1997, followed by Erin McKean. I grieved when it ceased publication in 2008, for I thought it the best of all language magazines. No language miscellany would be complete without acknowledging its extraordinary diversity, with contributions from all the leading word-enthusiasts of its day. Its articles would feed a dozen miscellanies, and indeed its last editor has produced one: *Verbatim: From the Bawdy to the Sublime, the Best Writing on Language for Word Lovers, Grammar Mavens, and Armchair Linguists* (2001).

So, as a bow to its unique presence, I've included five *Verbatim*-prompted pieces in this book. This one is from the first issue. American linguist Roger W Westcott wrote a piece that he called 'Word Chains in English' – phrases that follow a 'rule of three'. Each item contains only three words or word-like forms, never more than three syllables in length, and linked by sound repetition. He claimed the topic had never been noticed in English language studies before, and I think he was right. They include meaningful pieces of wisdom, nursery rhymes, commercial or political slogans, song refrains, nonsensical baby-talk, and general playfulness. Here are ten examples:

healthy, wealthy, and wise
shiver, quiver, and quake
hickory, dickory, dock
snap, crackle, and pop
cheery, beery, bee
rub-a-dub-dub
hot diggety dog
abba-dabba-doo
oobie-doobie-doo
kitchy-kitchy-koo

Those are all from the 1970s or earlier. The pattern is still with us:

better, greener, faster
dream, believe, succeed
see it, say it, sorted

More from early issues of ***Verbatim*** on pp. 75, 119, 167.

Lingua prancas – 1

IN 2010, the *New York* magazine had a competition in which you had to take a well-known expression in a foreign language, change or add a single letter, and provide a definition for the new expression. As I was running a blog at the time, I reported the winners, and it generated the largest amount of lexical inventiveness I've ever had, with over a thousand suggestions. To illustrate, I select expressions from that outpouring which are often used in English:

aide memwire	Will somebody please help me change this plug? [*aide memoire*]
anno domino	It's taken me a year to use my double six. [*anno domini*]
bon boyage	happy peripatetic scoutmaster [*bon voyage*]
dad nauseam	a grumpy old man [*ad nauseam*]
et netera	superfluous online content [*et cetera*]
faux pad	The flat has no original features. [*faux pas*]
modus hoperandi	At work, I have several sites to visit, so I use a pogo stick. [*modus operandi*]
nun sequitur	I'm not sure why, but she's giving up the habit. [*non sequitur*]
past de deux	We used to be an intimate couple. [*pas de deux*]
rainon d'être	The sudden realization you should have brought an umbrella. [*raison d'être*]

More **lingua prancas** on pp. 105, 157.

Car numbers

FINDING names, words, and general significance in car licence plates seems to be a universal pastime among car-owners. They may even influence literary creativity. Graham Greene was evidently a case in point. In a letter from Evelyn Waugh to Nancy Mitford, he tells her that, when Greene came to visit him, he would go into the nearby village and make notes of number plates, looking out for unusual combinations and reading meanings into them. It appears he had to do this before he could settle down to writing. Waugh elsewhere commented: 'He could not write another word until a certain combination of numbers – I think it was 987, something like that – appeared to him by accident.' Greene's novelist character Maurice Bendrix does something similar in *The End of the Affair* (1951):

> I've been so bored I've even collected car numbers. That teaches you about coincidences. Ten thousand possible numbers and God knows how many combinations, and yet over and over again I've seen two cars with the same figures side by side in a traffic block.

Tom Brown 1 – on conversations

IN 1699, satirist Tom Brown (1662–1704) published a series of 'colloquies', supposedly translations from Erasmus – hence the Latinate names. He calls one 'The Impertinents, or the Cross Purposes', as he explains in his preface:

> Two odd ill-contrived Fellows meet one another in the Street, and to talking they fall; one has his Head full of a Marriage, and the other's Thoughts run upon a Storm: In short, they Discourse with great Concern on both sides, and make nothing on't, only they fulfil the English Proverb between them, I talk of Chalk, and you of Cheese.

ANNIUS: Why? I hear you were Drunk as Lords all of you at Neighbour what d'ye call him's Wedding yesterday.

LUCIUS: The Duce take me if ever I knew such confounded Weather at Sea, tho' I have used it from my Cradle.

ANNIUS: So I find you had a world of brave Folks to see the Ceremony

LUCIUS: Fore George, (you make me Swear now) I never ran such a risque of drowning in my life before.

ANNIUS: Ay, ay, see what 'tis to be Rich, at my Wedding, tho' I sent again and again to all my Neighbours, yet only some half a dozen wou'd come near me, and those but sorry Wretches, the Lord knows.

LUCIUS: Mind me, I say, we were no sooner got off of the Land's end, but it blow'd as if it wou'd blow the Devil's Head off.

ANNIUS: God so! that was wonderful pretty, and were there then so many fine Lords and Ladies to throw the Stocking?[1]

LUCIUS: Comes me immediately a sudden Gust of Wind, and whips off the Sail, while you cou'd drink a Can of Flipp,[2] and tears it into a thousand Flitters, I warrant ye.

ANNIUS: You need not describe the Bride to me. Why? Lord, I knew the pretty Baggage when she was no taller than -

LUCIUS: Souse comes another Wave and runs away with the Rudder.

---

1 An old tradition, like the practice today of throwing a bouquet at a wedding

2 A new kind of drink in Brown's lifetime – a mixture of beer, rum and sugar, heated with a hot iron that caused the drink to froth (or 'flip').

And so it continues until they decide to go their different ways, apparently both satisfied with the conversation they've had together.

For more **Tom Brown**, see pp. 85, 185, 208.

Dickens' linguistic portraits – 1

MRS Merdle in *Little Dorrit* (1857):

> In the grammar of Mrs Merdle's verbs on this momentous subject, there was only one mood, the Imperative; and that Mood had only one Tense, the Present. Mrs Merdle's verbs were so pressingly presented to Mr Merdle to conjugate, that his sluggish blood and his long coat-cuffs became quite agitated.

More **linguistic portraits** on pp. 62, 106, 169, 186.

Expressions that never made it

IN 1788, the Anglo-Irish satirist Jonathan Swift (1667–1745) published the book that today is usually called *Polite Conversation* – its full title being *A Compleat Collection of Genteel and Ingenious Conversation, according to the most polite Mode and Method now used at Court, and in the best Companies of England, in several dialogues.* We are then treated to three conversations between seven upper-class ladies and gentlemen of the time, packed with the fashionable slang of the day. Several, such as 'Talk of the devil' and 'You can't see the wood for the trees', are still with us. Here are a dozen that aren't:

His grandmother and mine had four elbows. [*We are very good friends.*]
Butter is gold in the morning, and silver at noon, but lead at night. [*Its supposed effects on the stomach*]
Your tongue runs upon wheels this morning. [*You're very talkative.*]
The parson always christens his own child first. [*Charity begins at home.*]
Stand out of my spitting place. [*Stand out of my light.*]
Don't put tricks upon travellers. [*Don't make fools of us by telling us false tales.*]
My belly begins to cry cupboard. [*I'm very hungry.*]
London is gone out of town. [*Grown tremendously*]

My service to you. [*Cheers!*]
To be at the top of the house before the stairs are built. [*To run before you can walk*]
Your love's a million. [*You're much too kind.*]
Hold your tongue and mind your knitting. [*Mind your own business.*]

Collecting collectives – 2

MORE possibilities for collective nouns:

a clamber of roofers
a cloud of websites
a cogitation of intellectuals
a collection of postal workers
a column of journalists
a commission of sins
a company of friends
a complement of clauses
a contemplation of mystics
a conundrum of crosswords
a copse of policemen
a crop of hairdressers

Other **collectives** on pp. 3, 66, 133, 181.

The dangers of lexicography

ERIC Partridge (1894–1979) was the compiler of *A Dictionary of Slang and Unconventional English* (1937) and many other word-books. The most intriguing, to my mind, was his *Dictionary of the Underworld, British and American* (1950). Where did he get this information? This is what he says in his memoir *The Gentle Art of Lexicography* (1963):

> I met and, indeed, knew several crooks while I was serving in the AIF [Australian Imperial Force] during the First World War. I've listened to cant being spoken by groups of crooks and their hangers-on and by groups of petty and potential crooks: the flashy fellows of the race-course gangs and the urban gangs, the bludgers [pimps] and the lairs [flashy dressers], the look-out men (cockatoos) and the others. They were sure that I didn't understand a word they said and it's quite true that at first I didn't. I did, however, come to assimilate far more than they suspected.
>
> I was enabled, at no risk whatsoever, to establish contact with five or six crooks or knowledgeable 'near-crooks' and, for a beer or two, a half-crown here and there, to obtain certain information I needed.

He adds: 'One could, I suppose, fairly say that *Underworld* is an exciting work – but not to be read by the sensitive.'

Swifties

TOM Swift was a character created in a series of adventure novels, written by various authors under the pseudonym of Victor Appleton, beginning in 1910, with over a hundred titles in several series, some still appearing a century later. One feature of the dramatic style led to a new genre of linguistic humour, in the tradition of Wellerisms (p. 16), consisting of three parts: something Tom says, the reporting verb and his name, and an adverb ending in *-ly* (or sometimes a short adverbial phrase). Here are some examples from the opening chapter of one of the first books, *Tom Swift and His Airship* (1910):

> 'Shut it off!' cried Tom quickly.
> 'I don't bet,' replied Tom calmly.
> 'I don't know that it's any of your business,' Tom came back at him sharply.
> 'Yes, there was a small explosion,' admitted Tom, with a smile.

American writer Willard Espy (1911–99) saw the humorous potential, and exploited it in his various wordplay books with the name 'Tom Swifties'. It became a game, in which people were given the last part and invited to create an apposite first part.

> 'I couldn't get any apples,' said Tom fruitlessly.
> 'Is that the local cemetery?' Tom asked gravely.

'Look at the lambs gambolling!' said Tom sheepishly.
'I'm a terrible shot with a rifle,' said Tom aimlessly.
'This cream's off,' said Tom sourly.

There are also abbreviated versions, where the focus is on the verb:

'Can I become a chorister,' Tom inquired.
'I telephoned you twice,' Tom recalled.

Grammar as fun

THERE were several attempts in the Victorian era to make grammar interesting and amusing. One such case was published in 1840 by English satirist Percival Leigh (1813–89), and illustrated by John Leech (1817–64), *The Comic English Grammar*, described as 'a new and facetious introduction to the English tongue'.

A good example of Leigh's approach is in the chapter on etymology, where he points out gaps in the gender system. Having distinguished between a *cock-lobster* and a *hen-lobster*, and other male/female forms, he continues:

> We have heard it said that every Jack has his Jill. That may be; but it is by no means true that every cock has his hen; for there is
> Cock-swain, but no Hen-swain.
> Cock-eye, but no Hen-eye.
> Cock-ade, but no Hen-ade.
> Cock-atrice, but no Hen-atrice.
> Cock-horse, but no Hen-horse.
> Cock-ney but no Hen-ney.
> Then we have a weather-cock, but no weather-hen; a turn-cock, but no turn-hen; and many a jolly cock, but not one jolly hen; unless we except some of those by whom their mates are pecked.

English inn-names – 1

THERE were 50 tavern-names recorded by a curious observer who walked along the road from Whitehall to the Tower of London during the reign of James I (1603–25). That's a distance of just over 2 miles. So there was a hostelry every 70 yards or so. The spellings and abbreviations (y^e = the, S = Saint) are of the period, with the Roman numeral iij for 3.

> On the way from Whitehall to Charing Cross we pass the *White Hart*, the *Red Lion*, the *Mairmade*, *iij Tuns*, *Salutation*, the *Graihound*, the *Bell*, the *Golden Lyon*. In sight of Charing Cross: the *Garter*, the *Crown*, the *Bear & Ragged Staffe*, the *Angel*, the *King Henry Head*. Then from Charing Cross towards ye citti: another *White Hart*, the *Eagle & Child*, the *Helmet*, the *Swan*, the *Bell*, *King Harry Head*, the *Flower-de-Luce*, *Angel*, the *Holy Lambe*, the *Bear & Harroe*, the *Plough*, the *Shippe*, the *Black Bell*, another *King Harry Head*, the *Bull Head*, the *Golden Bull*, 'a sixpenny ordinarie',[1] another *Flower-de-Luce*, the *Red Lyon*, the *Horns*, the *White Hors*, the *Prince's Arms*, *Bell Savadge's In*, the *S. John the Baptist*, the *Talbot*, the *Shipp of War*, the *S. Dunstan*, the *Hercules* or the *Owld Man Tavern*, the *Mitar*, another *iij Tunnes Inn* and a *iij Tunes Tavern*, and a *Graihound*, another *Mitar*, another *King Harry Head*, *iij Tunnes*, and the *iij Cranes*.

---

1 A tavern where meals were provided at a fixed price.

For more **inn-names**, see pp. 138, 208.

A Victorian univocalic - *E*

IN 1824, Henry Vassall-Fox, 3rd Baron Holland (1773–1840), wrote a story of around 500 words, 'Eve's Legend', in which the only vowel used is *e*. Can it sound at all natural? You be the judge. Here's a short extract as he introduces the Vere family:

> The keen Peter, when free, wedded Hester Green – the slender, stern, severe, erect Hester Green. The next, clever Ned, less dependent, wedded sweet Ellen Heber. Stephen, ere he met the gentle Eve, never felt tenderness: he kept kennels, bred steeds, rested where the deer fed, went where green trees, where fresh breezes, greeted sleep. There he met the meek, the gentle Eve: she tended her sheep, she ever neglected self: she never heeded pelf[1], yet she heeded the shepherds even less. Nevertheless, her cheek reddened when she met Stephen ...

1 *Pelf* is an unusual word: it's from Old French and means 'money, riches'.

For other **univocalics**, see pp. 2, 80, 120, 171.

Literally ...

WHEN translators turn idioms from a foreign language into English, they naturally focus on their meaning, not their literal form. American writer Jag Bhalla looked at foreign idioms from the opposite point of view, as his book title illustrates: *I'm Not Hanging Noodles on Your Ears* (2009) is the Russian equivalent of 'I'm not pulling your leg'. He brought together over a thousand examples, such as these colourful expressions:

to be happy as castanets [Spanish] = to be ecstatic
to feel poodle-well [German] = to be on top of the world
to look like September [Russian] = to have a long face
to be like a dog in a canoe [Puerto Rican Spanish] = to be very nervous
camel-hearted [Hindi] = timid
the end is musk [Arabic] = a happy ending
have a fly on the nose [Italian] = have a chip on the shoulder
standing on one leg? [Yiddish] = in a hurry?
to cut a hair in four [French] = to split hairs
when snakes wore vests [Chilean Spanish] = a long time ago
be a Buddhist priest for three days [Japanese] = be a quitter
a face full of spring air [Chinese] = radiant with happiness

And one from me from Wales:

teach a parson the Lord's Prayer = teach your grandmother to suck eggs

Lockdown 1 – weakdays

THE COVID-19 pandemic stimulated a great deal of humorous linguistic invention – presumably arising from the tradition of laughing in the face of adversity. As lockdown continued, people seemed no longer to have any idea which day of the week was which, or what to do with them. Renaming was one proposed solution.

Moanday
Chooseday
Whensday
Blursday
Freeday
Satallday
Someday

For more **lockdown** coinages,
see pp. 54, 87, 121, 162, 199.

Being – 1

THE remarkable regional variations in England in the use of the verb *to be* were revealed by the Survey of English Dialects, carried out by a team under Harold Orton at the University of Leeds (1950–61), and published in *The Linguistic Atlas of England* in 1978. Informants from 313 locations all over England answered questionnaires that provided information about pronunciation, grammar, and vocabulary. A form such as standard English *I'm not* was found to have 15 regional variants:

I's not	I isn't	I baan't
I'm none	I aren't	I ben't,
I ain't	I ammet	I byen't,
I en't	I amno'	I byun't
I yun't	I bain't	I binno

That's just for England. If the search is broadened to other parts of the English-speaking world, more versions emerge, such as *I amn't*, and many variations in pronunciation.

For other examples of ***be* variation**, adapted from my *The Story of Be* (2017), see pp. 107, 197.

How much, did you say? – 2

AN obscure unit of currency, to modern eyes and ears, often mentioned in Shakespeare's plays, was the *mark*. In some countries this was the name of a coin, but in England it was only an accounting unit, with the value of two-thirds of a pound (160 old pence). Some goods were priced in marks, just as today a horse race might be priced in guineas. A mark would often be 'translated' into a coin currency, as in Act 2 of *King John*, where the king provides Blanche with a generous dowry:

KING JOHN: Then do I give Volquessen, Touraine,
Maine,
Poitiers and Anjou, these five provinces,
With her to thee; and this addition more,
Full thirty thousand marks of English coin.
Philip of France, if thou be pleased withal,
Command thy son and daughter to join hands.
King Philip: It likes us well.

I'm sure it does. If £1 Elizabethan = £100 today, John is offering him £20,000 – a cool £2 million.

For other **How much ...?**, see pp. 10, 92, 144, 205.

A word-change astonishing wrestle

THE Enigma, the magazine of the American National Puzzlers' League, was founded in 1883, and is still going. In 1936, it published a fine example of transpositional poetry, a sonnet by American lexicographer David Shulman (1912–2004), with anomalies corrected in a later issue. This is poetry in which each line is a rearrangement of the same letters – 29, in this case. He called it 'Washington Crossing the Delaware'. It's a hugely difficult challenge, especially if you want the lines to rhyme as well!

A hard, howling, tossing, water scene
Strong tide was washing hero clean.
'How cold!' Weather stings as in anger,
O silent night shows war ace danger!

The cold waters swashing on in rage,
Redcoats warn slow his hint engage.
When general's star action wish'd 'Go!'
He saw his ragged continentals row.

Ah, he stands – sailor crew went going,
And so this general watches rowing,
He hastens – Winter again grows cold;
A wet crew gain Hessian stronghold.

George can't lose war with's hands in;
He's astern – so, go alight, crew, and win!

Proposals from *Punch* - 1

MR Punch, in the very first volume of his magazine (July 1841), introduced a new way of printing stories, which he called stenotypography, and which he hoped would contribute to the success of his publication.* He illustrated with an extract from a romance about a lady and her two lovers, and helpfully added notes to aid readers unused to the names of printing symbols.

> Fitzorphandale had invited Seraphina to a picnic party. He had opened the &[1] placed some boiled beef and ‸‸[2] on the verdant grass, when Seraphina exclaimed, in the mildest of ´`,[3] 'I like it well done, Fitzorphandale!' As Julian proceeded to supply his beloved one with a §[4] of the provender, St. Tomkins stood before them with a †[5] in his ☞.

1. Hampers-and   *2. Carets*   *3. Accents*
4. Section   *5. Dagger*

* It evidently didn't, as he never used the system again.

For more ***Punch* proposals**, see pp. 93, 151, 198.

Word Ways remembered – 1

THE amazing periodical *Word Ways* was founded by German-American writer Dmitri Borgmann (1927–85) in 1968. It was subtitled *The Journal of Recreational Linguistics* and entirely devoted to wordplay. It sadly ceased publication in 2020, but an archive is available at the home of its last editor, Butler University: https://digitalcommons.butler.edu/wordways/all_issues.html

One of the best palindromic sequences – where each line reads the same from left to right and from right to left – ever was created by J A Lindon, from Weybridge, Surrey, in issue 4 of 1970:

In Eden

ADAM: Madam
EVE: Oh, who -
ADAM: (No girl-rig on)
EVE: Heh?
ADAM: Madam, I'm Adam.

EVE: Name of a foeman?
ADAM: O stone me! Not so.
EVE: Mad! A maid I am, Adam.
ADAM: Pure, eh? Called Ella? Cheer up.
EVE: Eve, not Ella. Brat-star ballet on? Eve.

ADAM: Eve?

EVE: Eve, maiden name. Both sad in Eden? I dash to be manned,
I am Eve.

And so it continues for over 50 more lines.

For more ***Word Ways* remembered**, see pp. 113, 190.

Usage – 1

OVERHEARD in a classroom. Mary, aged six, had just drawn a humanoid picture. 'That's a lovely big man, isn't it?' commented the teacher. To which Mary replied:

> If it was a lady, he might have a skirt on, mightn't she?

She may be only six, but adults can find themselves in a similarly uncertain position, especially given the greater sensitivity around the use of gendered pronouns these days. That final tag question is where speakers feel most unsure. Faced with a sentence that begins 'He's a woman ...', how is it to end? With 'isn't he?' or 'isn't she?'? Or is the issue to be sidestepped with 'isn't it?'? I've heard all three in recent times.

For other **usage** issues, see pp. 123, 170, 195.

Dickens' voice portraits – 2

RALPH Nickleby in *Nicholas Nickleby* (1839):

> If an iron door could be supposed to quarrel with its hinges, and to make a firm resolution to open with slow obstinacy, and grind them to powder in the process, it would emit a pleasanter sound in so doing, than did these words in the rough and bitter voice in which they were uttered by Ralph.

Other **voice portraits** on pp. 6, 84, 147, 204.

Wright's words – 1

JOSEPH Wright was recording words for his *English Dialect Dictionary* (p. 8) that were known in various parts of Britain during the late 19th century. Could it be that some are still known in some part of the country, or abroad? And even if they really have been lost, might people see their value and start using them again? Very often the old word expresses a meaning that no modern word does so well. And several have an appealing phonetic ring.

> Do you have a feeling that is a mixture of pricking and tingling? Try *prinkling*, recorded in Northumberland and Scotland. Or to trample lightly? Try *pample*, from East Anglia. And what about *graunch* (a blend of grind + crunch), *flimp* (flabby + limp), and *solemncholy* (solemn + melancholy)? They're all *capadocious* ('splendid'), as they used to say in Devon. Or, if you're feeling confused – in a state of *confloption* (East Anglia) – you might prefer *bamfoozled*, *beraffled*, *betwattled*, *bogfoundered*, *cabobbled*, *cumpuffled*, or *discomfrontled*.

If you want to explore further, the entire dictionary is now searchable online, thanks to a labour of love by scholars at the University of Innsbruck: https://eddonline4-proj.uibk.ac.at/edd/

For other words from the *English Dialect Dictionary*, see pp. 8, 81, 134, 188.

I don't get it - 1

SOME jokes work only in particular accents:

What's a metaphor?

A place for cows.

Say to that to someone in Britain, and there is blank incomprehension. The joke works only in American English, where the [t] is flapped and sounds more like a [d]. If you translate the first part of the word as 'meadow', you'll get it.

For another **I don't get it**, see p. 175.

Proverbial wisdom – 2

MORE proverbs translated into English from around the world, from my *As They Say in Zanzibar* (2006). This group is all to do with naming.

Good painters need not give a name to their pictures; bad ones must. [Poland]
A name doesn't harm us if we don't harm the name. [Estonia]
A dog with money is addressed as 'Mr Dog'. [USA]
Don't call the alligator a big-mouth till you have crossed the river. [Belize]
Bad is called good when worse happens. [Norway]
Good silence is called saintliness. [Portugal]
When you are chased by a wolf you call the boar your uncle. [Slovenia]
You come with a cat and call it a rabbit. [Cameroon]
The beginning of wisdom is to call things by their right names. [China]
Proverbs are so called because they are proved. [Italy]

And from England:

Call a spade a spade.

For other examples of **proverbial wisdom**, see pp. 12, 104, 156, 182.

Going global – 1

TWENTY entries from Lise Winer's *Dictionary of the English/Creole of Trinidad & Tobago* (p. 19), with glosses:

a bad moon with a belly ache	said of someone who's stubborn or who doesn't take advice
a brain like a fizz	said of someone who's distracted, unable to think properly (from the sound of bubbles coming out of a bottle)
that won't change the price of cocoa or coffee	it won't make the slightest difference
cool your brain(s)	relax, calm down
dance top in mud	try to do something impossible or too difficult (a top won't spin in mud)
eat like curry barb wire	said of someone in a very bad temper
finger and ring	said of two people who are always together, or very close
eat parrot head/tongue	said of someone who talks too much
that's half-pick duck	that's not the whole story – from taking only half the feathers off
have brother in mango tree	be very well connected

that's house and land	describing an exceptionally large object, such as a huge umbrella
lie like flatfish	said of someone who tells enormous continuous lies (stretching out the truth, in the way a flatfish lies very close to the ground)
make skylark	said of someone fooling around or being irresponsible
monkey say cool breeze	said to counsel patience (your time will come)
don't put cockroach before fowl	don't put temptation in someone's way
don't put water in your mouth	don't hold back from saying something
rain can't wet	said of someone who won't change their mind
we need to take night to make day	we need to make an all-out effort
even wet paper could cut you	everything is going wrong for you
what jail is this?	said when you find yourself in an unexpectedly difficult situation

For more **Going global**, see pp. 103, 143, 177, 194.

Lockdown 2 – zooming in

LOCKDOWN brought a flurry of new words relating to the growing popularity of platforms such as Zoom:

zoombie	the zombie-like state when someone leaves an overlong online meeting
zoombombing	an unexpected or unwelcome appearance during a Zoom meeting (on analogy with photobombing)
zoom coma	the state of lethargy that follows a long session in a Zoom room
zoomdate	a relationship formed after meeting someone in a Zoom room or other online forum
zoomed out or *zoomed up*	exhausted by spending too much time in Zoom rooms
zoomer	a member of Generation Z who lives life chiefly in Zoom rooms or other online meeting places
zoomped or *zumped*	the ending of a relationship formed in a Zoom room or other online forum

For other **lockdown** coinages, see pp. 40, 87, 121, 162, 199.

The mother of all words

IN 2004, the British Council marked its 70th anniversary with a survey. It asked 40,000 people in 102 non-English-speaking countries which was the most beautiful word in English. The top ten are shown below. It looks as if people chose their words on the basis of their meaning. When asked to focus on the sound alone, a different list would emerge. Individual authors have some interesting favourites, too (p. 57).

1. mother
2. passion
3. smile
4. love
5. eternity
6. fantastic
7. destiny
8. freedom
9. liberty
10. tranquillity

Peace came in at No. 11.

All you need is –

A survey of favourite words was conducted in 2007 by UK telecommuncations company Openreach, on behalf of the charity I Can, which helps children with communication difficulties. Fifty thousand people sent in their words in the first week of March and created a 'wall of words', which resulted in a donation of £50,000 to the charity. The word that came out top was *love*, followed by *serendipity*, *family*, *sunshine*, and *chocolate*. But there were many regional differences. In Scotland, the top word was one describing general foolishness, *numpty*. People were asked to say why they chose their word, and a surprising number of people gave the Beatles song as their reason for the top choice.

There's another **word survey** on p. 55.

Dylan's drome

DYLAN Thomas commented on his favourite words in a letter to English novelist Pamela Hansford Johnson written on Christmas Day 1933:

> I read in an old John O'London (blast the tit-bitty paper) several individual lists of favourite words, and was surprised to see that the choice depended almost entirely upon the associations of the words. 'Chime', 'melody', 'golden', 'silver', 'alive', etc. appeared in almost every list; 'chime', is, to me, the only word of that lot that can, intrinsically and minus its associations, be called beautiful. The greatest single word I know is 'drome' which, for some reason, nearly opens the doors of heaven for me. Say it yourself, out aloud, and see if you hear the golden gates swing backward as the last, long sound of the 'm' fades away. 'Drome', 'bone', 'dome', 'doom', 'province', 'dwell', 'prove', 'dolomite' – these are only a few of my favourite words, which are insufferably beautiful to me. The first four words are visionary; God moves in a long 'o'.

She must have sent him some words in reply, because in his next letter he writes: 'What beautiful words are "legend" & "island"; they shall certainly go on my list. But Ruth is the loveliest name.'

A lexicon of laughter

In 2008, the publishers of the *Chambers Dictionary* published a *Gigglossary* – a selection of the humorous definitions that had been a feature of their dictionaries since their first edition in 1901. They weren't the first to do this. Dr Johnson has several tongue-in-cheek entries in his 1755 *Dictionary*, such as *fishing*: 'a stick and a string, with a worm at one end and a fool at the other'. But no lexicographers have matched the ingenuity of the Chambers editors in their various editions (dates shown below). Here are ten of their entries:

baby-sitter	one who mounts guard over a baby to relieve the usual attendant [1952]
channel-surf	to switch rapidly between different television channels in a forlorn attempt to find anything of interest [2003]
comfort food	mood-enhancing food that meets the approval of one's taste buds but not of one's doctor [2008]
end-reader	one who peeps at the end of a novel to see if she got him [1952]
flag day	a day on which collectors solicit contributions to a charity in exchange for small flags as badges to secure immunity for the rest of the day [1901]

jaywalker	a careless pedestrian whom motorists are expected to avoid running down [1952]
middle age	between youth and old age, variously reckoned to suit the reckoner [1952]
perpetrate	to commit or execute (especially an offence, a poem, or a pun) [1962]
Santa Claus	an improbable source of improbable benefits [1972]
tracksuit	a loose warm suit intended to be worn by athletes when warming up or training, but sometimes worn by others in an error of judgment [2003]

The practice was widely noticed and appreciated, as a welcome departure from the normally staid tone of dictionary definitions, so much so that in 2003 the firm opened its online doors to readers to supply further examples, and added more creations of its own. Four more from that list:

accountant	a person who will prove that two and two did make four, but, after deducting professional fees, now only comes to three
birthday cake	a consolation prize awarded annually
cat	a partially domesticated animal who keeps you as a pet
recommendation	a name generally used for the highest-priced dish on any menu

Could they have said it?

ONE of the most difficult tasks for a historical dramatist or novelist is to get the language of the time right. Researchers can spend an age establishing points of dress, table manners, and so on, especially for a TV drama, but fail to check that the slang given to the characters is appropriate. Here's a selection of real or possible anachronisms from the first series of *Downton Abbey* (2010), set in April 1912. The numbers in parentheses refer to the episodes; the dates are those of the first recorded usage in the *Oxford English Dictionary*. It is of course possible that there are earlier unrecorded usages.

Clear cases

O'Brien says 'that's Her Greatness done and dusted for the night' – a colloquial idiom not recorded until 1953. (4)

Mary says Sybil was 'banging on about her new frock' – not recorded until 1979. (4)

William has paid Mrs Hughes a compliment, who responds by saying: 'Stop flannelling and get on' – a slang use, meaning 'flatter', not recorded until 1941. (4)

Gwen asks Anna if she hid her absence from the others: 'Did you cover for me?' – a sense (covering up for an employee) not recorded until 1968. (5)

Lady Violet suggests a foreign husband for Mary: 'You can normally find an Italian who isn't too picky.' Meaning 'fastidious', very colloquial, first recorded in 1957. (6)

Possible cases

Matthew describes a pair of cufflinks as 'a bit fiddly' – not recorded until 1926. (2)

Evelyn describes his horse as being 'as jumpy as a deb at her first ball' – an abbreviation not recorded until 1922. (3)

Would English people have used these Americanisms?

Thomas tells O'Brien: 'Don't be such a grouch' – recorded in the US in 1901. (5)

Marty tells Matthew that Sybil has discovered politics, 'which of course makes Papa see red'. Recorded in the US in 1901. (6)

Gwen tells Sybil: 'Forgive me, m'lady, but you don't get it.' Recorded in the US in 1926. (6)

How to avoid anachronisms? First step: go to the online *OED*, and especially its *Historical Thesaurus*. Second step: read as much period literature as possible (which is of course what the *OED* researchers have done, over the years).

Dickens' linguistic portraits – 2

Mr Pecksniff in *Martin Chuzzlewit* (1844):

> Mr Pecksniff's manner was so bland, and he nodded his head so soothingly, and showed in everything such an affable sense of his own excellence, that anybody would have been ... comforted by the mere voice and presence of such a man; and though he had merely said 'a verb must agree with its nominative case in number and person, my good friend' ... must have felt deeply grateful to him for his humanity and wisdom.

Other **linguistic portraits** on pp. 29, 106, 169, 186.

Perverbs

THIS blend of *pervert* and *proverb* identifies a language game where the aim is to make a new expression by combining the first half of one proverb with the second half of another. As in these examples:

The road to hell is paved with rolling stones.
A bird in the hand makes the most noise.
An apple a day is the mother of invention.
Too many cooks make light work.
A new broom gathers no moss.
A stitch in time keeps the doctor away.
A watched pot is in the eye of the beholder.
Don't throw the baby out while the sun shines.
Early to bed and early to rise makes Jack a dull boy.
If at first you don't succeed, get out of the kitchen.
The more things change, the harder they fall.

Comic alphabets – 2

Eric Partridge, in his historical and copiously illustrated *Comic Alphabets* (1961), thought that the following example was the best of the genre, and I agree. It was a romantic tale compiled by C S Calverley (1831–84) in 1862.

A is an Angel of blushing eighteen;
B is the ball where the Angel was seen;
C is her Chaperon, who cheated at cards;
D is the Deuxtemps[1] with Frank of the Guards;
E is her eye, killing slowly but surely;
F is the fan, whence it peeped so demurely;
G is the Glove of superlative kid;
H is the Hand which it spitefully hid;
I is the Ice which the fair one demanded;
J is the Juvenile, that dainty who handed;
K is the Kerchief, a rare work of art;
L is the Lace which composed the chief part;
M is the old Maid who watch'd the chits dance;
N is the Nose she turned up at each glance;
O is the Olga[2] (just then in its prime);
P is the Partner who wouldn't keep time;
Q's a Quadrille, put instead of the Lancers;[3]
R the Remonstrances made by the dancers;
S is the Supper, where all went in pairs;
T is the Twaddle they talked on the stairs;
U is the Uncle who 'thought we'd be goin'';

V is the Voice which his niece replied 'No' in;
W is the Waiter, who sat up till eight;
X is his Exit, not rigidly straight;
Y is a Yawning Fit caused by the ball;
Z stands for Zero, or nothing at all.

---

1 'Two-time': a more rapid waltz than the ordinary three-beat waltz.

2 Partridge thought this was a dance of Slavic origin, perhaps related to the mazurka.

3 A very fashionable dance in mid-Victorian times, the latest variant of the normal quadrille (presumably why the dancers remonstrate).

For other **comic alphabets**, see pp. 9, 135, 179, 202.

Collecting collectives - 3

STILL more possibilities for collective nouns:

a deceit of impostors
a delivery of midwives
a digest of restaurant critics
a discourse of phoneticians
a drift of snowploughs
a fabrication of storytellers
a file of programmers
a flood of plumbers
a fragrance of florists
a galaxy of astronomers
a gambit of chess masters
a grid of electricians

Other **collectives** on pp. 3, 32, 133, 181.

&

NOT many graphic symbols inspire poetry, but this one did, in *Punch* magazine (17 April 1869). The author remains anonymous. It's a lengthy epic. Here are three of its stanzas:

> Of all the types in a printer's hand
> Commend me to the Amperzand,[1]
> For he's the gentleman, (seems to me)
> Of the typographical companie.
> O my nice little Amperzand,
> My graceful, swanlike Amperzand,
> Nothing that Cadmus ever planned
> Equals my elegant Amperzand!
>
> He's never bothered, like A.B.C.
> In Index, Guide, and Directorie:
> He's never stuck on a Peeler's[2] coat,
> Nor hung to show where the folks must vote.
> No, my nice little Amperzand,
> My plump and curly Amperzand
> When I've a pen in a listless hand,
> I'm always making an Amperzand!
>
> But he is dear in old friendship's call,
> Or when love is laughing through lady-scrawl:
> 'Come & dine, & have bachelor's fare.'
> 'Come, & I'll keep you a Round & Square.'[3]

Yes, my nice little Amperzand
Never must into a word expand,
Gentle sign of affection stand,
My kind, familiar Amperzand,

---

1 The *z* spelling was quite common during the 19th century.

2 A *peeler* was a policeman.

3 A *round and square* alludes to a slice of beef.

A Biercian alphabetical selection

THE *Devil's Dictionary* (1911) by Ambrose Bierce (1842–*c.* 1914) was begun as a column in a weekly paper in 1881 and continued with intervals until 1906. The first, shorter 1906 edition was titled *The Cynic's Word Book*, and his cynical humour shines through every one of the thousand or so entries that appeared in 1911. Later research by Ernest J Hopkins brought to light over 800 previously unpublished entries, and *The Enlarged Devil's Dictionary* came out in 1967, from which the following selection is taken:

admiration n. Our polite recognition of another's resemblance to ourselves.

bard n A person who makes rhymes. The word is one of the numerous aliases under which the poet seeks to veil his identity and escape opprobrium.

consolation n. The knowledge that a better man is more unfortunate than yourself.

demented n. The melancholy mental condition of one whose arguments we are unable to answer.

envelope n. The coffin of a document; the scabbard of a bill; the husk of a remittance; the bed-gown of a love-letter.

fault n. One of my offenses, as distinguished from one of yours, the latter being crimes.

guilt n.	The condition of one who is known to have committed an indiscretion, as distinguished from the state of him who has covered his tracks.
heaven n.	A place where the wicked cease from troubling you with talk of their personal affairs, and the good listen with attention while you expound your own.
ignoramus n.	A person unacquainted with certain kinds of knowledge familiar to yourself, and having certain other kinds that you know nothing about.
joy n.	An emotion variously excited, but in its highest degree arising from the contemplation of grief in another.
kindness n.	A brief preface to ten volumes of exaction.
lecturer n.	One with his hand in your pocket, his tongue in your ear and his faith in your patience.
magic n.	The art of converting superstition into coin.
novel n.	A short story padded.
omen n.	A sign that something will happen if nothing happens.
patience n.	A minor form of despair, disguised as a virtue.
quantity n.	A good substitute for quality, when you are hungry.
railroad n.	The chief of many mechanical devices enabling us to get away from where we are to where we are no better off.
scribbler n.	A professional writer whose views are antagonistic to one's own.

telephone n.	An invention of the devil which abrogates some of the advantages of making a disagreeable person keep his distance.
ultimatum n.	In diplomacy, a last demand before resorting to concessions.
valor n.	A soldierly compound of vanity, duty and the gambler's hope.
weather n.	The climate of an hour.
X	in our alphabet being a needless letter has an added invincibility to the attacks of the spelling reformers, and like them, will probably last as long as the language.
year n.	A period of three hundred and sixty-five disappointments.
zeal n.	A certain nervous disorder afflicting the young and inexperienced. A passion that goeth before a sprawl.

For more **Ambrose Bierce**, see pp. 145, 196.

Why Snowtober won

IN 2011, there was a media debate in the USA about the best term to describe an unexpected snowstorm in October. *Snowtober*, *Octsnowber*, and *Snoctober* had all been suggested. *Snowtober* won. Why? I think *Octsnowber* lost out because it buried the crucial word in the middle of the month, and the combination of four consonants *ctsn* was unappealing. And *Snoctober* turned the long vowel into a short one – *snoc* – so that the immediate link with *snow* disappears. *Snowtober* nicely avoided these problems.

A Shakespearean find

IN the traditional spirit of the first of April, I celebrated the tenth anniversary of Shakespeare's Globe in 2007 by gifting it my discovery of a lost quarto of *Hamlet*, which showed that Shakespeare suffered from octoliteraphilia – an obsession with the eighth letter of the alphabet, which he was usually able to control, but evidently not entirely. The entire manuscript, known as the *H Quarto*, was later published on 1 April 2016 to mark the 400th anniversary of his death, titled *The Unbelievable Hamlet Discovery*. The beginning of the play is reproduced here:

Hamlet headquarters

BARNARDO: Hark!

FRANCISCO: Ho! Henchman?

BARNARDO: He.

FRANCISCO: Hey, hour heedfully heeded.

BARNARDO: Horological halfnight's happened. Hop home.

FRANCISCO: Hokay. Horrendously heartless. Heartsick.

BARNARDO: Have had harmony here?

FRANCISCO: Housemice have hushed.

Horatio / Marcellus hither

HORATIO: Hello.

MARCELLUS: Holla.

BARNARDO: Horatio!

HORATIO: H-h-half here.

MARCELLUS: Hamlet henchmen have had horrible haunting.

HORATIO: Humph!

BARNARDO: Heck! Hair-raising hackles have happened. Heebie-jeebies. Horrible.

HORATIO: Hallucinations, henchmen. Had hallucinogens?

BARNARDO: Haven't had hashish.

HORATIO: Have.

FRANCISCO: Haven't

HORATIO: Humbug! Hangovers? Headaches?

Haunter hither

MARCELLUS: Hellfire! Horrendous haunter's hovering hither.

And so it continues until the final lines of the tragedy, spoken by Hardarms (Fortinbras):

Hearse honourable Hamlet! Hoist him high.
Ho, henchmen. Have hardware hit heavens!

Hexeunt

There was an unexpected sequel: p. 191.

Incontrovertible

IN the first issue of *Verbatim* (see pp. 23–4) in 1982, Norman Schur brought together a huge number of adjectives whose negative forms are far more frequent than their positive counterparts. Indeed, in many cases, there's no positive counterpart at all. Some are quite well known, such as *unkempt* and *disgruntled*, but I don't recall anyone compiling so full a collection before – well over a hundred instances. Here are a dozen from his list of adjectives prefixed with *im-* or *in-*:

imperturbable	inescapable
impervious	inevitable
imponderable	inextricable
incalculable	innumerable
incongruous	inscrutable
ineffable	insuperable

He thought his readers would enjoy the exercise of changing negative words to their positive forms to see what happens. This is his sample sentence (with a suffix thrown in for good measure):

> The ungainly fellow, despite his unheard-of unnerving and unsettling experience, managed in some unfathomable way to behave unimpeachably in his uncompromising, unswerving, dauntless determination to put an unceremonious end to the indescribably unconscionable, nay unmentionable misdeeds of his implacable antagonist.

The queerest thing

MARK Twain wrote a piece for *Atlantic Monthly* (1 June 1880), just four years after the telephone had been invented. He thought: 'a conversation by telephone – when you are simply sitting by and not taking any part in that conversation – is one of the solemnest curiosities of this modern life.' He reports his experience of listening to one such call. It is, he says:

> that queerest of all the queer things in this world, – a conversation with only one end to it. You hear questions asked; you don't hear the answer. You hear invitations given; you hear no thanks in return. You have listening pauses of dead silence, followed by apparently irrelevant and unjustifiable exclamations of glad surprise, or sorrow, or dismay. You can't make head or tail of the talk, because you never hear anything that the person at the other end of the wire says. Well, I heard the following remarkable series of observations, all from the one tongue, and all shouted.
>
> Yes? Why, how did *that* happen?
> *Pause.*
> What did you say?
> *Pause.*
> Oh, no, I don't think it was.
> *Pause.*

No! Oh, no, I didn't mean *that*. I meant, put it in while it is still boiling, – or just before it *comes* to a boil.

Pause.

WHAT?

Pause.

I turned it over with a back stitch on the selvage edge.

Pause.

Yes, I like that way, too; but I think it's better to baste it on with Valenciennes or bombazine, or something of that sort. It gives it such an air, – and attracts so much notice.

Pause.

It's forty-ninth Deuteronomy, sixty-fourth to ninety-seventh inclusive. I think we ought all to read it often.

Pause.

Perhaps so; I generally use a hair-pin.

Pause.

What did you say? [*Aside*] Children, do be quiet!

Pause.

Oh! B *flat*! Dear me, I thought you said it was the cat!

Pause.

Since *when*?

Pause.

Why, *I* never heard of it.

Pause.

You astound me! It seems utterly impossible!

Pause.

Who did?

Pause.

Good-ness gracious!

Pause.

Well, what *is* this world coming to? Was it right in *church*?

Pause.

And was her *mother* there?

And so it continues. If the exercise were repeated today, I doubt much would have changed.

The taming of the shrew?

On 6 January 2016, in the House of Commons, the Conservative member for Stratford-upon-Avon, Nadhim Zahawi, suggested to the Prime Minister, David Cameron, that the country should unite to commemorate the works of Shakespeare during the 400th anniversary of his death. The PM agreed and went on:

> I find that Shakespeare provides language for every moment. Let us consider what we are thinking about at the moment. There was a moment when it looked like this reshuffle [in the Labour Party shadow cabinet, led at the time by Jeremy Corbyn] could go into its twelfth night. It was a revenge reshuffle, so it was going to be as you like it. I think, though, we can conclude that it has turned into something of a comedy of errors – perhaps much ado about nothing. There will be those who worry that love's Labour's lost.

A Victorian univocalic – *I*

THESE lines were titled 'The Approach of Evening':

Idling, I sit in this mild twilight dim,
Whilst birds, in wild, swift vigils, circling skim,
Light winds in sighing sink, till, rising bright,
Night's Virgin pilgrim swims in vivid light!

For other **univocalics**, see pp. 2, 38, 120, 171.

Wright's words - 2

HERE are some of the words from Joseph Wright's *English Dialect Dictionary* (p. 8) that I selected for inclusion in my celebratory book *The Disappearing Dictionary* (2015):

dabberlick (*noun*) Known in Scotland, especially Banffshire and Nairnshire.

A mildly insulting way of talking about someone who is tall and skinny. 'Where's that dabberlick of a child?' The word was also used for long stringy seaweed, for ragged clothing, and for hair that hangs down in tangled and separate locks.

dottled [*adjective*] Known in Scotland and Lincolnshire.

Said of anyone acting in a silly, foolish, or confused way. 'If I hadn't been so dottled I'd've thought of that!' The word was especially used to talk about someone apparently in a state of dotage. 'The poor chap's gone quite dottled.'

fubsy [*adjective*] Known in Lancashire and Yorkshire.

Plump, in a nice sort of way. Rudyard Kipling liked this word. In *The Jungle Book* (1894), Baloo uses it in one of his laws of the jungle:

> Oppress not the cubs of the stranger, but hail them as Sister and Brother,
> For though they are little and fubsy, it may be the Bear is their mother.

Stephen Fry liked it, too, and in 2009 adopted this word as part of a 'Save the Last Word' campaign for HarperCollins English Dictionaries.

rickmatick [*noun*] Known in parts of Scotland and Ireland.

A concern or affair, or a collection of something. 'I sent off the whole rickmatick to the cleaner's.' 'He brought the whole rickmatick clattering down on the floor.' As these examples suggest, people usually talked about 'the whole rickmatick'.

smittling [*adjective*] Known in Lincolnshire, Lancashire, Yorkshire, and further north.

Contagious, infectious. 'The sickness must be something smittling, for it's gone through everyone in the house.' You would also hear it described as smittleish.

squinch [*noun*] Known in Devon and throughout the West Country of England

A narrow crack in a wall or a space between floorboards. 'I lost a pound through a squinch in the floor.' A long narrow window might be called a squinch, too.

For other words from ***The Disappearing Dictionary***, see pp. 134, 188.

Anagramming

ALL wordplay enthusiasts love to find apposite anagrams, as shown in *Telegram* (p. 21) and from contributors to *Enigma* over the years, and they became a regular source of crossword clues. Some examples from its first 60 years:

greyhound – hey, dog, run! (1898)
negation – gets a 'no' in (1926)
decimal point – I'm a dot in place (1928)
incomprehensible – problem in Chinese (1929)
cabaret – a bar, etc (1941)
inconsistent – n is, n is not, etc (1943)

Linguistics terminology proves remarkably resistant to anagrammatisation, probably because so much of it contains infrequent or repeated letters, as in *syntax*, *grammar*, *lexicography*, *vocabulary*, *phonology*, *linguistics* ... But don't let me stop you trying.

Dickens' voice portraits – 3

SIR Leicester Dedlock in *Bleak House* (1852):

> His voice was rich and mellow; and he had so long been thoroughly persuaded of the weight and import to mankind of any word he said, that his words really had come to sound as if there were something in them.

Other **voice portraits** on pp. 6, 48, 147, 204.

Tom Brown 2 – on poetry

In 1699, satirist Tom Brown wrote a letter 'To a young Lawyer that dabbl'd in Poetry' – what he calls the 'rhyming disease'. He advises him not to go down that path, in terms that remain just as relevant today.

> Law and Poetry are as incompatible as War and Plenty, and that the Lawyer and Poet can no more inhabit in the same person, than a Beau and a Chimney-sweeper. The Law proposeth interest for its end, and that consideration makes its Thistles palatable; but you'll find your self damnably mistaken, if you think to advance your self by the Muses. After you have spent your whole age in their service, you must not expect to have your Arrears paid so much as in Malt-Tickets, or Exchequer-Notes.[1] They'll put you off to one Mrs *Tattle* alias *Fame*, the veryest Coquette that ever was, and that prating Gossip will sham you with an Immortality-Ticket forsooth, which is not to become due to you, till you are laid asleep in a Church-yard; and neither you, nor your Heirs will be a farthing the better for it.

And he concludes:

> So then, if you have the fear of Interest before your eyes, stick close to the Law, and let Poetry go the Devil.

---

1 Two parliamentary initiatives. The malt lottery was promoted in 1697, with malt duty as security. An exchequer-note was a bill of credit first issued in 1696, bearing interest at the current rate. Brown evidently didn't think much of them.

For more **Tom Brown**, see pp. 27, 185, 208.

Lockdown 3 – Covidese

THE *cov* syllable at the beginning of the name *COVID* generated a huge number of puns and neologisms:

covads	television and other commercials made at home or selling virus-related products
coventine	a quarantined nunnery
covexit	the elimination of the COVID-19 virus in a country, and maybe, one day, the world
covictory	the anticipated situation when the virus is finally brought under control
covidalliance	a relationship born online during a period of lockdown or at a distance while outside
Covidentry, sent to	made to leave a social group because of a fear that the person has the virus
covideo	a home video made during lockdown
covidese	the vocabulary created in 2020 to laugh in the face of the virus
covidiot	the usual term of abuse for anyone thought to be breaching lockdown guidelines; the condemned behaviour is *covidiocy*
covidivorce	the likely outcome for a married couple who haven't survived the pressure of self-isolation

covidodge	a sudden movement to avoid coming into contact with a passer-by during a period of social distancing; also called a *covid waltz*
covidreaming	vivid or nightmarish dreams experienced during a virus lockdown, such as seeing yourself unable to get into a restaurant while everyone else is eating inside
coviduals	people (individuals) who devise a creative approach to coping at home
covidiversity	an online institution offering academic courses while universities are closed
covipet	an animal obtained to give the owner a permissible reason to leave the house; many kinds, such as *covicats*, *covidogs*, and *coviparrots*
coviewing	watching a movie or other show online along with others in different houses
covignette	a small design or anecdote circulated online to keep spirits up
covigorousness	the state of keeping extra-busy during lockdown
covilla	a rather nice second home, especially abroad, which is now unreachable
covillain	someone who takes advantage of the crisis to commit crimes
covindaloo	an unexpectedly hot takeaway ordered during lockdown
covindictive	taking one's COVID-related frustrations out on others

covincible	a personal belief that one is immune from the virus
covindicated	the state following an antibody test, positive or negative
covintage	wine produced during 2020
covirginity	a state of enforced chastity due to lockdown
covirility	the male feeling of 'it's not going to get ME'
covitroll	an online vitriol-spreading covidiot
covocabulary	new words and senses that describe the COVID-19 event

For other **lockdown** coinages,
see pp. 40, 54, 121, 162, 199.

A proverb poem

THIS cheeky sonnet was penned by Michael Drayton (1563–1631).

As Love and I late harbour'd in one inn,
With Proverbs thus each other entertain:
'In love there is no lack,' thus I begin;
'Fair words make fools,' replieth he again;
'Who spares to speak doth spare to speed,' quoth I;
'As well,' saith he, 'too forward as too slow;'
'Fortune assists the boldest,' I reply;
'A hasty man,' quoth he, 'ne'er wanted woe;'
'Labour is light where love,' quoth I, 'doth pay;'
Saith he, 'Light burden's heavy, if far borne;'
Quoth I, 'The main lost, cast the by away;'
'Y'have spun a fair thread,' he replies in scorn.
And having thus awhile each other thwarted,
Fools as we met, so fools again we parted.

A punctuated relationship

I was sent this example of a modern equivocation (p. 4):

> Dear Eric,
> I want a man who knows what love is all about. You are generous, kind, thoughtful. People who are not like you admit to being useless and inferior. You have ruined me for other men. I yearn for you. I have no feelings whatsoever when we're apart. I can be forever happy – will you let me be yours?
> Mary.

> Dear Eric,
> I want a man who knows what love is. All about you are generous, kind, thoughtful people, who are not like you. Admit to being useless and inferior. You have ruined me. For other men, I yearn. For you, I have no feelings whatsoever. When we're apart, I can be forever happy. Will you let me be?
> Yours. Mary

Playing with punctuation in this way has a long history, with examples dating from medieval times. A famous Elizabethan instance is the way Peter Quince gets things wrong in a speech in Act 5 of Shakespeare's *A Midsummer Night's Dream*, leading Duke Theseus to comment: 'This fellow does not stand upon points.'

How much, did you say? – 3

AN obscure unit of currency in Shakespeare's plays was the *ducat*. This was a gold (sometimes a silver) coin used in some European countries, especially Italy. Its value varied, but usually it was worth between a fifth and a third of an English pound – overlapping with the value of a crown. So when Antonio wants a loan of 3,000 ducats from Shylock, in Act 1 of *The Merchant of Venice*, that would be about £75,000 in modern money – a sufficiently large sum to make Shylock think twice ('Well ... Well ...').

On that basis, Shylock is understandably upset at the sums lost via his daughter:

> A diamond gone, cost me two thousand ducats in Frankfurt!

That's £50,000 today. And Jessica is quite a gambler, it seems:

> Tubal: Your daughter spent in Genoa, as I heard, one night fourscore ducats.
> Shylock: Thou stick'st a dagger in me. I shall never see my gold again. Fourscore ducats at a sitting, fourscore ducats!

That would be £2,000 down the drain today.

For other **How much ...?**, see pp. 10, 42, 144, 205.

Proposals from *Punch* - 2

IN Volume 3 of his magazine (1843), Mr Punch recommends the setting up of libraries for the police. He is upset that the force should have 'so little acquaintance with letters', and he continues:

> But so it is, for in vain do we endeavour to constitute our Police force a really lettered body, if, with vowels on their cuffs, consonants on their collars, mutes on their lanterns, and liquids – too frequently – in their mouths, we do not engrave Grammar on their hearts, and imprint Syntax on their memories.
>
> It may be asked, how is education to aid a policeman in the discharge of his duty? We gladly take up the anonymous gauntlet by answering the question in the usual way – by putting another. How is a policeman to interfere with confidence in a dispute between man and wife, if he is not aware of the true force of the copulative conjunction?

For other ***Punch* proposals**, see pp. 44, 151, 198.

A laughing matter

WHY do people laugh? The expected answer is: because something is funny. But when all the instances of laughter in a large collection of conversation recordings are analysed, it turns out that only a minority are caused by humour. Most are in response to what someone has just said.

The laugh of sympathy – I hear what you're saying and I'm enjoying it.
The laugh of disbelief – I hear what you're saying and you can't be serious; you're kidding me.
The laugh of embarrassment – I hear what you're saying and it's making me feel uncomfortable.
The laugh of awkwardness – I hear what you're saying and I'm finding that really difficult to respond to.
The laugh of rejection – I hear what you're saying and there's no way I'm going to comment (very common in media interviews).
The laugh of surrender – I've no idea what to say about that.

Some are self-comments:

The laugh of empathy – I know I'm saying something unpleasant and I hope you don't mind.
The laugh of avoidance – I realise I'm saying something tricky so I want to move on to a different topic.

The laugh of apology – I realise I've just used a sensitive or taboo word, and I hope it's not offended you.
The laugh of incompleteness – I don't need to finish my sentence as I'm sure you can see what I'm trying to say.
The laugh of finishing a topic – I'm done – very common in online chat, especially with LOL (p. 96).

Lolling

LOL – the online acronym for 'laughing out loud' – rarely means what it says, so much so that when a message *does* actually make someone laugh out loud, they feel they need to qualify it, and say 'actual LOL', or the like. So why is LOL used? Studies of collections of emails and texts suggest that, when responding to a message, it usually means 'I've enjoyed hearing what you've just said'. But more often, it points up something in one's own message.

After a remark, to mean 'I'm kidding'.
After a remark, to mean 'I'm especially happy about what I've just said'.
At various points in a message to mean 'I hope you like what I'm saying'.
At the end of a sentence to signal a change of topic.
At the end of a message to signal 'It's your turn to talk now'.

It's not the commonest sign of humour. 'Haha' and its variants are much more frequent than LOL or emoticons, especially among older messagers.

Descriptions – 1

OF Tobias Achilles Lempriere's mode of speaking, in Richard Flanagan's novel *Gould's Book of Fish* (2001, p. 108):

> Words existed in his speech as currants in a badly made bread-and-butter pudding – clusters of stodgy darkness.

For more **descriptions**, see pp. 128, 176.

Nashisms

THE most ingenious rhymer of the 20th century, many think – and I agree – was the American poet Ogden Nash (1902–71), acclaimed for his humorous writing and unconventional line-endings. Here are some couplets from his early (1930s) collections:

What would you do if you were up a dark alley and
there was Caesar Borgia.
And he was coming torgia.

Let us pause to consider the English,
Who when they pause to consider themselves they
get all reticently thrilled and tinglish.

The caveman had to get up before he could go out and
track the brontosaurus.
Verdi had to get up before he could sit down and compose the Anvil Chorus.

Does anybody mind if I don't live in a house that is
quaint?
Because for one thing, quaint houses are generally
houses where plumbing ain't.

Many beautiful thoughts have been thought about
Autumn,
And many distinguished people have thautumn.

And a linguistic one:

> Seated one day at the dictionary I was pretty weary
> and also pretty ill at ease,

This is a typical Nash strategy: he sets up a situation and, in effect, dares the reader to predict where he's going to go next. He then follows it up with a second dare, creating a line-ending where it might seem impossible to achieve a rhyme – but of course he always finds one.

> Because a word I had always liked turned out not to be a
> word at all, and suddenly I found myself among the v's.
> And suddenly among the v's I came across a new word
> which was a word called *velleity*.
> So the new word I found was better than the old word
> I lost, for which I thank my tutelary deity.

It's not easy to emulate Nashisms. To show this, here are a few examples of a Nash line-ending. Can you provide a plausible rhyme? (Non-standard spellings allowed, of course.) Nash's choices are on p. 217.

avenue insouciance cavalry cobra metaphor
Scandinavia Sahara

No way

If you want to express disbelief about what someone has just said, it's often not enough to say simply 'no' or 'never', and studies of conversation have found a range of colourful expressions of strong denial. Curiously, these are often preceded by a 'yeah', and never by the negative conjunction *but*. The *yeah* has to be said with a dismissive intonation, of course.

in your dreams
what planet are you on
when pigs fly
and I'm a monkey's uncle
and I'm the Queen of Sheba
and my Uncle Joe has hair
when hell freezes over

A reference to any very distant, inaccessible, or fictional place can add extra force, such as Timbuktu or Planet Crap. The exact phrasing can vary, but the impact is the same.

Echo verse

THIS ingenious poetic genre was especially popular in the 17th century, and continues to attract writers. The following example dates from 1634: a dialogue between a glutton and a condemnatory echo. These are the opening exchanges:

GLUTTON: My belly I do deifie.
ECHO: Fie!
GLUTTON: Who curb's his appetite's a fool.
ECHO: Ah fool!
GLUTTON: I do not like this abstinence.
ECHO: Hence!
GLUTTON: My joy's a feast, my wish is wine.
ECHO: Swine.
GLUTTON: We epicures are happie truly.
ECHO: You lie.
GLUTTON: Who's that which giveth me the lie?
ECHO: I.

And so it continues, with Glutton giving some warnings:

GLUTTON: Wilt hurt me if I drink too much?
ECHO: Much.
GLUTTON: Thou mock'st me, nymph; I'll not believe it.
ECHO: Believe it.

GLUTTON: Is't this which brings infirmities?
ECHO: It is.
GLUTTON: Whither will't bring my soul? canst tell?
ECHO: T'hell.

Eventually he sees the error of his ways:

GLUTTON: Wouldst have me temperate till I die?
ECHO: Ay.
GLUTTON: Shall I therein find ease and pleasure?
ECHO: Yea, sure.
GLUTTON: Will it my life on earth prolong?
ECHO: Oh, long!
GLUTTON: Will't bring me to eternal bliss?
ECHO: Yes.
GLUTTON: Then, sweetest Temperance, I'll love thee.
ECHO: I love thee.

Going global - 2

IN 2016, Jean Branford and Michael Venter published a collection of essays on expressions that have taken on a new meaning in South African English. They called it *Say Again?* Here are some examples:

eat with long teeth	eat unwillingly or without enjoyment
a when-we	naming anyone who's always talking about the 'good old days', 'when we ... '
pavement specials	mongrel dogs or cats of no clear breed, presumably conceived on the street
a monkey's wedding	the simultaneous occurrence of sunshine and rain
hold thumbs	to bring good luck or avoid harm, as 'cross fingers'
have a cadenza	be extremely agitated about something – possibly from Danny Kaye's 1948 children's recording, 'The Lost Fiddle', where a fiddle 'gets so excited that he has a big cadenza'.

For more **Going global**, see pp. 52, 143, 177, 194.

Proverbial wisdom - 3

MORE proverbs translated into English from around the world, from my *As They Say in Zanzibar* (2006). This group is all to do with speech.

It is easier to speak than to say something. [Ukraine]
Speak of the miracle, but don't mention the saint. [Philippines]
Turn your tongue seven times before speaking. [France]
Wine and children speak the truth. [Romania]
Those who speak much must either know a lot or lie a lot. [Germany]
Speak, lest tomorrow you be prevented. [Kenya]
An untouched drum does not speak. [Liberia]
Slander by the stream will be heard by the frogs. [Mozambique]
A crow in a cage won't talk like a parrot. [USA]
Who speaks of it commits it not. [Italy]

And from the UK:

Many a true word is spoken in jest.
Speech is silver; silence is golden.
Dead men tell no tales.

For other examples of **proverbial wisdom**, see pp. 12, 51, 156, 182.

Lingua prancas – 2

MORE contributions to my blog challenge, where one has to choose a well-known expression in a foreign language, change or add a single letter, and provide a definition for the new expression.

For some reason, food and drink phrases attracted dozens of suggestions, such as ...

add hoc	Don't forget the wine. [*ad hoc*]
café au late	They're taking a long time with the coffee. [*café au lait*]
Château-eneuf-du-Pape	Surely the pope has sufficient real estate. [*Châteauneuf-du-Pape*]
coq au van	We're getting a home delivery of poultry. [*coq au vin*]
Côtes du Phone	I've left my mobile on the beach. [*Côtes du Rhône*]
crème brûleg	The ointment's working on my lower limb. [*crème brûlée*]
tea culpa	Actually, I'd prefer coffee. [*mea culpa*]
vain rouge	I certainly have no problem being a redhead. [*vin rouge*]
bone appétit	a dog's dinner [*bon appétit*]
bun appétit	Hope you like the cake. [*bon appétit*]

Other **lingua prancas** on pp. 25, 157.

Dickens' linguistic portraits – 3

MR Squeers in *Nicholas Nickleby* (1839):

> PEG: Is that you?
>
> SQUEERS: Ah, it's me, and me's the first person singular, nominative case, agreeing with the verb it's, and governed by Squeers understood, as a acorn, a hour; but when the h is sounded, the a only is to be used, as a and, a art, a ighway. At least, if it isn't, you don't know any better. And if it is, I've done it accidentally.

Other **linguistic portraits** on pp. 29, 62, 169, 186.

Being – 2

SINCE the 17th century, *you are* has become the only accepted form for the second-person singular in standard English. Speakers and writers of that variety encounter *thou art* only in a small range of distinctive settings, such as prayers, the Bible, Shakespeare, and imaginative reconstructions of the speech of such characters as Robin Hood, King Arthur, variegated pirates, and the medieval heroes of innumerable children's comics.

But in regional dialects, these forms are in competition with several other popular forms. One group clusters around variants of *be*: *you bist*, *bees*, *beest*, *beost*, and *bes*, as well as *been*, *ben*, and *beth*. Often there's a contrast in meaning, with *are/art* conveying a one-off event, and forms based on *be* used for a habitual activity:

you are on the ferry –	I can see you are
you be on the ferry –	you work on board a ferry

In the north of England and in Scotland, people have been recorded as saying *thou is* and *you is*, and this usage turns up in various parts of the English-speaking world, especially in the Caribbean and the American South.

Another Southern regionalism for this form of the verb is *you em* or *am*. It seems that any form of the verb *be* can be used as the second person: *thou/you am*, *are/art*, *is*. And the same diversity appears in the regional variants when abbreviated. We see such forms as *you'm*, *thou'rt*, *thou're*, *thou's*, and *you's* alongside the modern informal standard *you're*.

For other examples of ***be* variation**, see pp. 41, 197.

Speak the speech

IN 1910, the American dictionary company Funk & Wagnalls published a small book called *Phrases for Public Speakers*, compiled by Grenville Kleiser (1868–1935), who wrote or compiled over 50 books on oratory and public speaking. This one, the title page states, was 'For the Exclusive Use of Grenville Kleiser's Mail Course Students'. In his introduction he explains how the book should be used: 'The student should read aloud daily several pages of these phrases, think just what each one means, and whenever possible fill out the phrase in his own words. A month's earnest practice of this kind will yield astonishing results.' There are nearly a thousand phrases in all. Here are those under letters *O* and *P*, which should provide enough opportunity for anyone uncertain of their public speaking eloquence to try it out.

Observe, if you please, that
Occasionally it is whispered that
Of course, it will be said that
Of no less import is
Of the final issue I have no doubt.
On the contrary

On the one hand
On the other hand
On the other hand, you will see
On the whole, then, I observe
Once more, how else could
One fact is clear

One word more and I have done.

Only a few days ago

Our position is that

Our position is unquestionable.

Over and over again it has been shown that

Perhaps, sir, I am mistaken in

Perhaps the reason of this may be

Permit me to add another circumstance.

Permit me to remind you

Please remember that if

Forgery?

IN an issue of *Babel* magazine in 2020, readers were set a challenge: to decide whether a piece of text purporting to be from a lost Shakespeare play was genuine. It has to be a forgery, as four of the words and three phrases in it were not yet in English, in Shakespeare's time.

John:
When I return with victory from the field,
I'll see your grace; but I will go to George
And meet him at th'hotel within the park,
For there he plans to eat and parle with me.

Elinor:
My darling boy, my sweetling, take thou care
If with him at his luncheon you do sit
For when he's full of drink, inebrious,
He's nothing to be trusted, and his wiles
Can trap a boy as innocent as thee.

John:
I fear not, mother, but will heed your word
I am no silly ass of George's kind.
And if he starts a broil to gain my end
I have the necess'ry to end his life.
He'll go to meet his maker ere I flee.

Elinor:
Stay yet awhile another day with me.
'Tis ugly weather to go out so far
And country paths are treach'rous in the wind.

See p. 218 for the answers.

! ? ! !

Word Ways remembered - 2

Ross Eckler, one of the editors of *Word Ways*, penned in 1986 what he thought would be an unbeatable literary isogram – a genre in which each word, rather than each letter, appears only once. It's easy to start, but it gets increasingly difficult as the text lengthens, because the grammatical words all get used up. And, as he says, it's a cheat just to add strings of adjectives, or the like (the sort of thing an artificial intelligence bot would do). He also points out that a decision has to be made about what kinds of words count – whether to allow all word forms (*a* as well as *an*), *horses* as well as *horse*, and hyphenated forms. It's difficult to write a text of more than a hundred words. Eckler manages 188 and leaves us with a challenge. (He explains his use of bold and underlining in the piece.)

Metalinguistic thoughts set down* at *random

Below, dear reader, you will encounter perhaps **the** longest English-language literary isogram ever constructed: every word therein **is** unique. While reading, please watch carefully **for** inadvertent duplications (hopefully, **they** appear impossible **to** find). Professor H.J. Verschuyl has written **a** considerably longer Dutch example (see Battus's *Opperlandse taal & letterkunde*, page 62); however, **this** work does **not** translate very felicitously. **Had he**, perchance, too many foreign idioms in his account?

Formerly, some writers piled **one** adjective **on** another ad nauseam, **but** such concatenation **was** often criticized **as** making humdrum narrative. My essay employs those 33 words (emphasized with boldface type) rated most common **by** Kucera **and** Francis.[1]

Note **that I have** used **an** article here – profligate wastefulness, because it may never **be** reused. Why underline these? Similarities among letter sequences raise perplexing questions; can prefixing legitimatize root reuse? What about changes **of** tense, shown above? **Or** plurals? Hyphenated terms cause additional problems; **are** their component parts disallowed? Clearly, different spellings must always generate admissible lexical forms.

Who shall write more extensive prose passages **which**, free **from** any repetition whatever, sound natural throughout?

1 Henry Kučera and W Nelson Francis, *Computational Analysis of Present-Day American English* (Brown University Press, 1967).

For other ***Word Ways*** **remembered**, see pp. 45, 190.

Unfinished proverbs

A number of proverbs become so well known in a culture that the user only has to say the first part, knowing that the listener can complete it in some shape or form. It's a pattern of usage that gives second-language learners real difficulty.

Ask a silly question ...
What the eye cannot see ...
If the cap fits ...
Those who laugh last ...
People who live in glass houses ...
The proof of the pudding ...
An apple a day ...
Many hands ...
If you scratch my back ...
A bird in the hand ...

The completions, if needed, are on p. 218.

Thank you – and then?

WHAT do you say when someone thanks you after providing you with a favour or a service? Recent studies in the field of pragmatics have shown there's a range of formulaic utterances and general responses, formal and casual, with varying nuances:

> You can express your happiness: *a pleasure*, *my pleasure*, *great pleasure.*
> You can express your absence of concern: *not at all*, *that's OK*, *that's all right*, *no problem*, *no trouble, no worries.*
> You can say the thanks is unnecessary: *don't mention it*, *don't worry about it.*
> You can express your appreciation that you had the opportunity to provide the service: *you're (very) welcome* (the favourite of restaurant staff).
> You can offer a repeat: *any time.*
> You can just make a positive noise: *of course*, *awesome*, *great*, *fantastic*, *cheers*, *you got it, absolutely*, *sure*, *yeah* (with an appropriate intonation).

Not all are universal. *OK* is much more likely in British English than in American English, for example. And fashions change. *You're welcome* used to be typically American, but is now widespread in the UK.

The importance of proofreading

SEVERAL books have been published with collections of typographical or other errors in newspapers – 'press boners' or 'bloopers' The following list shows some of the ones that turned up in proofs of the first edition of *The Cambridge Encyclopedia* (1990), but which were fortunately spotted before the book was signed off:

> Such works [of art] are intended to appal in their own right.
> Tatum ... continued to work in the [jazz] idiom until after his death.
> The Khoisan now live mainly in the Kalahari Dessert.
> This was his best-known bonk.
> The quantum hypothesis explained the observed rate of emission of radiation from hot bidies very well.

Then there were such phrases as these:

> Index of Prohibited Boos
> the beauty of Carolingian rat
> Vatican, a scared city
> Word War I ... World Wart II
> proper and common nuns

And some of the ones which it was tempting to leave ...

mewdicine [training for vets who specialise in cats?]
disagreenments [disputes over environmental policy?]
backruptcy [due to the cost of private surgery to correct a slipped disc?]
theatre of cruety [playwriting in which salt and pepper pots play a major role?]
nagazines [periodicals aimed at those whose relationships are breaking down?]
merdicine [for French doctors who specialise in gastro-intestinal problems?]

Take a gander

THE great American linguistic humourist Richard Lederer (1938–) wrote many articles for *Verbatim* (pp. 23–4). In the second issue for 1982 he brought together an extraordinary number of animal-related expressions in an article he called 'A visit to the language zoo'. As he says ...

> It's a dog-eat-dog world we live in – one unbridled rat race. And, doggone it, I do not wish to duck or leap-frog over this subject. It's time to fish or cut bait, to take the bull by the horns, and to give you a bird's-eye view of the animal metaphors in our language.

Which is what he does – over 200 of them. Here's a further flavour:

> I mean, holy cow, holy cats, and holy mackerel – the human race is filled with congressional hawks and doves who fight like cats and dogs, Wall Street bulls and bears who make a beeline for the goose that lays the golden egg, cold fish and hot doggers, early birds and night owls, lone wolves and social butterflies, and lame ducks, sitting ducks, and dead ducks. [...]
>
> Other people have a whale of an appetite that compels them to eat like pigs, drink like fishes, hog the lion's share, and wolf their elephantine portions until they become plump as partridges.

For more **Lederer**, see p. 167.

A Victorian univocalic - *O*

THESE lines were part of a long sequence headed 'Incontrovertible Facts':

No cool monsoons blow soft on Oxford dons,
Orthodox, jog-trot, book-worm Solomons!
Bold Ostrogoths, of ghosts no horror show,
On London shop-fronts no hop-blossoms grow.
To crocks of gold no dodo looks for food.
On soft cloth footstools no old fox doth brood.
Long storm-tost sloops forlorn, work to no port.
Rooks do not roost on spoons, nor woodcocks snort,
Nor dog on snow-drop or on coltsfoot rolls,
Nor common frogs concoct long protocols.

For other **univocalics**, see pp. 2, 38, 80, 171.

Lockdown 4 – quarantimes

THAT is how historians might one day label 2020. And the historical lexicographers will have a field day. Here's a top 20 based on *quarantine*.

quarantanned	how one looks, following an overuse of tanning equipment during lockdown
quaranteaching	what all teachers have to do while schools are closed
quaranteam	any group – sporting, musical, theatrical ... – performing together online
quaranteatime	meeting online to share a cup of tea during lockdown
quarantechnology	any device, physical or digital, that helps pass the time while staying at home during a lockdown; also *quarantech*
quarantedium	for many, the daily state
quarantee	the promise made by a government or other organization to do something to help people suffering financial loss during lockdown; also, the first drive in golf where the golfers have to maintain social distancing
quaranteen	a youngster who becomes a teenager in 2033
quaranteenager	there are few things more fearsome

quaranteeny	an infant no longer able to go to a crèche or nursery-school
quaranteething	of babies: first teeth coming through while in lockdown
quaranteetotal	giving up alcohol during lockdown
quarantime	the sense of timelessness while in lockdown
quarantini	a looked-forward-to Martini-type drink while having to stay at home
quarantip	any idea that helps you survive a period of lockdown
quarantipple	an increased reliance on alcohol during lockdown
quarantough	a description of the times we live in during lockdown
quarantrendy	describing any new fashion, recipe, game, exercise ... that becomes popular during lockdown
quarantunes	songs composed to raise spirits
quaranTV	television programmes or online videos being watched assiduously

For other **lockdown** coinages,
see pp. 40, 54, 87, 162, 199.

Usage – 2

IN this ever-changing world in which we live in

This is the famous fourth line of the Paul and Linda McCartney song 'Live and Let Die' (1973), as it appeared in the original sheet music. It wasn't long before the apparent ungrammaticality of the double *in* was noticed, and the suggestion made that the last word was actually *livin'*. On the other hand, it was pointed out that the prepositional construction was echoed in the next line: 'Makes you give in and cry'.

The solution? Ask the man. But when Paul was asked about it in a *Washington Post* interview, he was puzzled:

> Yeah, good question. It's kind of ambivalent, isn't it? ... Um ... I think it's 'in which we're living' ... Or it could be 'in which we live in.' And that's kind of, sort of, wronger but cuter.

He's right. Constructions where a preposition is inadvertently repeated are extremely common. Linguists call them 'syntactic blends'. Here are some examples from websites:

> For which party will you vote for in the March 9th election?
> We all have marriage role models, couples to which we look up to and aspire to be like.
> From which country does a Lexus come from?

Blends like these arise when people are (unconsciously) uncertain which of two competing constructions to use, so they use them both. In this case, the uncertainty arises because the traditional prescription against ending a sentence with a preposition pushes users to speak (or sing) formally, and we end up with 'in which ...'; whereas the natural rhythm of the language pulls them in another, more colloquial direction, and we end up with '... live in'. Personally, I vote for the latter.

For other **usage** issues, see pp. 47, 170, 195.

Skipping changes

IONA and Peter Opie, in *The Lore and Language of Schoolchildren* (1959), trace the development of a children's playground rhyme used for skipping or counting-out over 250 years. Their earliest instance is from 1725 (though the source is probably much older); their latest 1954. Here are six examples from the sequence, showing the way a theme (*forgot* and its rhyme) is maintained despite many changes. The sources are from widely different locations in England and Scotland.

1725

Now he acts the Grenadier
Calling for a Pot of Beer
Where's his Money? He's forgot:
Get him gone, a Drunken Sot.

1780

Who comes here?
A Grenadier.
What do you want?
A Pot of Beer.
Where is your money?
I've forgot.
Get you gone
You drunken Sot.

1916

Rat a tat tat, who is that?
Only grandma's pussy-cat.
What do you want?
A pint of milk.
Where is your money?
In my pocket.
Where is your pocket?
I forgot it.
O you silly pussy-cat.

1943

Rat tat tat, who is that?
Only Mrs Pussy Cat.
What do you want?
A pint of milk.
Where's your penny?
In my pocket.
Where's your pocket?
I forgot it.
Please walk out.

1952

A pig walked into a public house
And asked for a drink of beer.
Where's your money, sir?
In my pocket, sir.
Where's your pocket, sir?

In my jacket, sir.
Where's your jacket, sir?
I forgot it, sir.
Please walk out.

1954

I had a little beer shop
A man walked in.
I asked him what he wanted.
A bottle of gin.
Where's your money?
In my pocket.
Where's your pocket?
I forgot it.
Please walk out.

Descriptions - 2

MAYA Angelou's description of her father's voice in *I Know Why the Caged Bird Sings* (1969, Chapter 9, p. 54):

> His voice rang like a metal dipper hitting a bucket ...

For more **descriptions**, see pp. 97, 176.

Blending

LINGUISTIC blends, or 'portmanteau words', as Lewis Carroll's Humpty Dumpty calls them, became very popular during the 20th century, and coinages continue to flood in. Some hardly need glossing, but several have alternative meanings, depending on whether the first or the second element dominates.

abnormous [abnormal + enormous]	exceptionally large
bewilderness [bewilderment + wilderness]	total confusion
camerature [camera + caricature]	a deliberately manipulated photograph
daffynition [daffy + definition]	a humorous definition [as often in this book]
evidentually [evident + eventually]	something that will be clear in due course
flightseeing [flight + sightseeing]	tourism by helicopter, or the like
grandificent [grand + magnificent]	exceptionally splendid
horrorscope [horror + horoscope]	a horoscope predicting the worst

infomaniac [information + maniac]	anyone fascinated by trivia [as the author of this book, and possibly its readers]
jargantuan [jargon + gargantuan]	the scale of the task facing anyone trying to keep up with the latest jargon
kidult [kid + adult]	media watchers of an intermediate age
lumbersome [lumbering + cumbersome]	extremely awkward or ponderous
mirthquake [mirth + earthquake]	of someone shaking with laughter
nonsensational [nonsense + sensational]	an event thought to be unnecessarily overpraised
odditorium [odd + auditorium]	a place displaying oddities and curiosities [such as this book]
pushency [push + urgency]	demanding immediate attention
queuetopia [queue + utopia]	an imagined world where one queues for everything[1]
rendezwoo [rendezvous + woo]	a meeting place for lovers
scandiculous [scandalous + ridiculous]	absurd amount of attention given to a piece of juicy news
torrible [torrid + horrible]	of a highly unpleasant heatwave
ubookquitous [book + ubiquitous]	a bestseller

vidiot [video + idiot]	a video-game or video-watcher obsessive
wegotism [we + egotism]	anyone who uses the editorial 'we' too much
xpectacle [expectation + spectacle]	an anticipated great event [excuse the alphabetical cheat]
yumptious [yummy + scrumptious]	really delicious
zedonk [zebra + donkey]	the hybrid offspring of a zebra and a donkey

1 Actually coined by Winston Churchill in 1950: 'The socialist dream is no longer of Utopia, but Queuetopia.'

Nonsense verse

THE genre was popular in Victorian times and is well known today through the writing of Edward Lear and Lewis Carroll. Less known are the occasional pieces in the periodicals of the time, such as this one from *Fun*, a humorous magazine that aimed to compete with *Punch*, published between 1861 and 1901. It was called 'A Chronicle' and begins:

> Once – but no matter when -
> There lived – no matter where -
> A man, whose name – but then
> I need not that declare.
>
> He – well, he had been born,
> And so he was alive;
> His age – I details scorn -
> Was somethingty and five,
>
> He lived – how many years
> I truly can't decide;
> But this one fact appears
> He lived – until he died.

And so it continues, until its final stanza:

> MORAL
> In this brief pedigree
> A moral we should find -
> But what it ought to be
> Has quite escaped my mind.

Collecting collectives – 4

YET more possibilities for collective nouns:

a grumble of complaints
a harmony of choirs
a jam of tarts
a trunk of elephants
a knot of shoelaces
a litigation of lawyers
a lineage of ancestors
a leash of dog walkers
a number of mathematicians
a pack of suitcases
a pontification of pundits
a pray of priests

Other **collectives** on pp. 3, 32, 66, 181.

Wright's words – 3

MORE words from Joseph Wright's *English Dialect Dictionary* (p. 8):

backsyfore [*adjective or adverb*] Known in Devon, Cornwall, and Shropshire.
The wrong side first. 'You've put on your hat backsyfore.' Or 'clumsy'. It also gave rise to *backsyforemost* and the rhyming *backsyforsy*.

betwittered [*adjective*] Known in Yorkshire.
Anything that might cause you to *twitter* 'tremble' – be excited or frightened. Maybe this has already found a new lease of life in social media.

cheeping-merry [*adjective*] Known in Lancashire.
Half-drunk, feeling elevated – high, I suppose, also, today.

haveage [*noun*] Known in Devon and Cornwall.
Lineage, family stock. 'You can tell from her looks she's from a good haveage.' This is an unusual use of the verb *have* in its sense of 'come into possession of'.

slonky [*adjective*] Known in Ireland, Scotland, Northumberland, Kent – virtually anywhere, it would seem.
Having muddy places, or wet hollows. 'That road's really slonky.' *Slonk* is from Old English, referring to any sort of depression in the ground.

For other words from ***The Disappearing Dictionary***, see pp. 81, 188.

Comic alphabets – 3

THE genre was at its best when it told a story or expressed a point of view. This one from around 1890 was called simply 'Another Alphabet', and signed by 'Another Disappointed Author'.

A is an 'Andle to somebody's name;
B's for the Book that's writ by the same.
C's for the cheque that the 'andle commands;
D for the Difference left in my hands.
E's the Emolument for commoners fit;
F is the Fuss that they make about it.
G is the Gold that from authors' brains comes;
H is for Heaven that smiles on the sums.
I's for Insatiable; likewise Inept;
J's the shrewd Judgment that never has slept.
K is for Kontract that never was kept.
L's for Laus Deo,[1] in thanks for my gains;
M is for Money that smells not nor stains.
N is for Never was such a good man;
O is for 'Overs',[2] a capital plan;
P for the Power our trade-books to scan.
Q is for Quixote, the type of our band;
R's for the Records all ready to hand.
S for Successful attempts to look bland.
T's for the Troublesome creatures who say,

That 'Under this contract you really must pay.'
V for the Vengeance I'll compass one day;
W for Wanity,[3] apt to betray.
X, but for one objection, stands for Xerxes,
Y is because most limited my acquaintance with classical works is;
And with a Z, for all I know, may be the proper way to spell Zerxes.

1 Latin: 'Thanks [be] to God'.
2 A tax-accounting term for when cash receipts exceed recorded amounts.
3 A *w/v* alternation, apparently common in Victorian Cockney speech, and most famously recorded by Charles Dickens in the character of Sam Weller.

For other **comic alphabets**, see pp. 9, 64, 179, 202.

Old saws

In 1910, Walter William Skeat (1835–1912), Professor of Anglo-Saxon at Cambridge, also known for his work on Middle English, made a collection of English proverbial expressions he found in manuscripts of the 13th and 14th centuries. Here are a dozen that have not come down to us, though the meanings will have modern parallels:

Drink only with the duck. [i.e. water]
Often a full dexterous smith forges a very weak knife.
The cock is brave on his own dunghill.
The greater and higher the hill, the greater the wind on it.
The middle way of moderation is always golden.
He that does not when he may, shall not when he would.
When the cup is fullest, then carry it most carefully.
That which is cheaply bought brings a poor return.
No man can succeed by being speechless.
There are more stars than two.
Seldom is Friday like the other days in the week.
The thing that is said is said, and forth it goes.

English inn-names - 2

WHY tavern-names were so called was a continual puzzle, and led to many commentaries, such as this one by playwright Thomas Heywood (*c.* 1570s–1641) in 1608, suggesting that the names reflect the type of person who frequents them:

The Gintry to the Kings Head,
The Nobles to the Crown,
The Knights unto the Golden Fleece,
And to the Plough the Clowne.

The Churchmen to the Mitre,
The Shepheard to the Star,
The Gardener hies him to the Rose,
To the Drum the Man of War.

The Huntsmen to the White Hart,
To the Ship the Merchants goe,
But you that doe the Muses love,
The sign called River Po.

The Banquerout[1] to the World's End,
The Fool to the Fortune hie,
Unto the Mouth the Oyster-wife,
The Fiddler to the Pie.

The Punk[2] unto the Cockatrice,
The Drunkard to the Vine,
The Begger to the Bush, there meet,
And with Duke Humphrey dine.[3]

---

1 Bankrupt.

2 Prostitute.

3 The reference is to an aisle of Old St Paul's Cathedral, London, known as Duke Humphrey's Walk (after Humphrey, Duke of Gloucester, the brother of Henry V), frequented by people who couldn't afford a meal.

For other **inn-names**, see pp. 37, 208.

Word bluffing

THIS is a puzzle that's been on various television quiz shows, and which learners of English as a foreign language find especially intriguing – especially when they realise that native speakers of English have just as much difficulty as they do. The task is simple: which of the various definitions is the correct one? (Consulting a dictionary not allowed!)

LOADBERRY

1. A container for soft fruit in a supermarket: 'Put the strawberries in the loadberry.'
2. A type of birthmark: 'He hopes to get his loadberry removed surgically.'
3. A small, enclosed landing-place for the unloading of boats: 'The house had a loadberry attached.'
4. A kind of mobile phone with a special facility for downloading data: 'Have you seen the latest loadberry?'

BEEN-TO

1. The name of a travel brochure: 'Do you want the been-to for Greece?'
2. A ramshackle toilet outside a house: 'It was very cold in the been-to.'

3. A person who has travelled to England to be educated: 'From the way she talked you could tell she was a been-to.'
4. A log kept by the Royal Shakespeare Company of the plays Friends of the RSC have seen: 'According to the been-to, Mr Brown has seen six plays last year.'

COCKABULLY

1. A type of peaked hat: 'He wore his cockabully at a jaunty angle.'
2. A sexually arrogant male: 'I hate those cockabullies who are always trying to get off with you.'
3. A small blunt-nosed freshwater fish: 'The cockabully is a corruption of a Māori word, *kokopu*.'
4. A farmyard bird with many hens: 'He's a fine cockabully, strutting around.'

Answers, if needed, on p. 217.

Oxen, brethren, children, and that's it?

GRAMMARIANS always thought it was. The *-en* noun ending which marks a plural in English was no longer productive. Then along comes the internet, and the linguistic geeks decide to resuscitate it – but only for nouns ending in *-x*. So, in the late 1990s, we find:

vaxen, for VAX computer users
bixen, for BIX users (an information exchange system)
matrixen, for lots of matrixes
boxen, for lots of boxes

I haven't come across these coinages recently, but they may still be out there somewhere.

Going global - 3

In 1978, G A Wilkes published *A Dictionary of Australian Colloquialisms* – comprising a wide range of informal vocabulary and many colourful expressions, such as 'wet enough to bog a duck' (extremely wet) and 'busy as a one-armed milker on a dairy farm' (for a particularly slack day). Here are half a dozen that describe someone who – in the opinion of the speaker – is not very competent at performing a task:

couldn't find a grand piano in a one-roomed house
couldn't lead a flock of homing pigeons home
couldn't fight his/her way out of a paper bag
couldn't knock the skin off a rice pudding
couldn't tell the time if the town hall clock fell on him/her
as useless/useful as an ashtray on a motorbike

For more **Going global**, see pp. 52, 103, 177, 194.

How much, did you say? - 4

For the most impressive unit of all in Shakespeare's plays, we have to go to *Timon of Athens*, where we encounter the *talent*. This was a high-value accounting unit in some ancient countries, ultimately related to a large chunk of precious metal, such as silver. In ancient Greece it was the equivalent of around nine years' worth of wages for a skilled labourer working five days a week all year round

Transferring that to Shakespeare's time, where a labourer might earn around 10 pence a day, a talent was equivalent to about £100. A thousand talents would be some £100,000. So Timon, in Act 2, is being really demanding when he sends his servant to the senators with the instruction:

Bid 'em send o'th' instant
A thousand talents to me.

No wonder the senators turn him down!

For other **How much ...?**, see pp. 10, 42, 92, 205.

Bierce on language

A BAKER'S dozen of the entries on linguistic topics in Ambrose Bierce's *The Devil's Dictionary* (p. 69):

circumlocution n.	A literary trick whereby the writer who has nothing to say breaks it gently to the reader.
discussion n.	A method of confirming others in their errors.
eulogy n.	Praise of a person who has either the advantages of wealth and power, or the consideration to be dead.
fib n.	A lie that has not cut its teeth.
interpreter n.	One who enables two persons of different languages to understand each other by repeating to each what it would have been to the interpreter's advantage for the other to have said.
lexicographer n.	A pestilent fellow who, under the pretense of recording some particular stage in the development of a language, does what he can to arrest its growth, stiffen its flexibility and mechanize its methods.
linguist n.	A person more learned in the languages of others than wise in his own.

loquacity n.	A disorder which renders the sufferer unable to curb his tongue when you wish to talk.
me pron.	The objectionable case of *I*. The personal pronoun in English has three cases, the dominative, the objectionable and the oppressive. Each is all three.
monologue n.	The activity of a tongue that has no ears.
oratory n.	A conspiracy between speech and action to cheat the understanding.
positive adj.	Mistaken at the top of one's voice.
prevaricator n.	A liar in the caterpillar state.

For more **Ambrose Bierce**, see pp. 71, 196.

Dickens' voice portraits – 4

MRS Pardiggle in *Bleak House* (1852):

> She was a formidable style of lady, with spectacles, a prominent nose, and a loud voice, who had the effect of wanting a great deal of room. Always speaking in the same demonstrative, loud, hard tone, so that her voice impressed my fancy as if it had a set of spectacles on too.

Other **voice portraits** on pp. 6, 48, 84, 204.

Having a go

IN 1941, the news on the BBC was read for the first time by someone with a regional accent – Yorkshireman Wilfred Pickles, who would later become a household name for his long-running listener-participation show *Have a Go* (which gave the nation such catchphrases as 'What's on the table, Mabel?' and 'Give him the money, Barney'). In his autobiography, *Between You and Me* (1949), he tells us that he asked John Snagge (a famous BBC voice of the time) how this came about, and was told that the idea had come from Brendan Bracken, the Minister of Information, who had suggested 'a change of voice, as he feels listeners are getting a little tired of the so-called Oxford accent; and as a security measure because your accent might not be so easily copied by the Germans'.

He enjoyed the experience, despite the criticisms he received:

> When I read the midnight news, I remembered John Snagge's words, 'Do as you like,' and I rounded off the bulletin by bidding the listeners: 'Good night to you all – and to all Northerners wherever you may be, good neet!' This, it was later discovered, came as an especial pleasure and a link with home to the North-country lads serving in foreign parts, whether they were stationed in the Middle East or the South of England.

> I was ready for a rap from the B.B.C., but none came, and the first official reference to it was not made until two or three weeks afterwards when John Snagge said to me: 'We rather like your good neet!'

He received a huge fan mail:

> What was clear from the letters was that the lads from Leeds and Manchester and all-points north, south, east and west of those cities where the short 'a' was part of the dialect [as in *bath* vs *bahth*] found my voice brought them a comforting feeling that the old familiar places and faces were still there. While the praise came to me, the abuse poured into the postal section of the B.B.C. That short 'a' was the focus. The press had headlines such as 'Lahst a thing of the Pahst.'

The Listener Research Department of the BBC reassured him: they pointed out that 'people who wrote to the BBC did so because they were annoyed at a programme or something in a programme, but those who were impressed decided to write but never got round to it.' (I take reassurance from this too, as I received similar letters criticising my accent when I presented *English Now* on Radio 4 in the 1980s.)

Love counts

WHICH of Shakespeare's plays uses the word *love* and its main variants (*loves, loved, loving, lovest*) most? People usually opt for *Romeo and Juliet* (149 instances), but in fact that takes second place to *The Two Gentlemen of Verona* (189 instances). They're closely followed by *As You Like It* (140 instances). But the *Sonnets* beat them all, with 191.

And which plays use them least? Two tie: *The Tempest* and *The Comedy of Errors*, both with 20 instances, with *Macbeth* just ahead of them at 25. (The counts are based on the editions at www.shakespeareswords.com.)

Proposals from *Punch* - 3

In Volume 6 of his magazine (1844), Mr Punch proposes an Act for the Amendment of the Orthography of Surnames. It begins:

> Whereas divers and sundry persons, subjects of Her Most Gracious Majesty, Victoria, of Great Britain and Ireland Queen, Defender of the Faith, are known, called, and designated by certain surnames, which are spelt one way and pronounced another; and whereas such names are so spelt that nobody upon earth could, from their spelling, have the remotest idea of the pronunciation; by reason where of, others, faithful subjects of Her said Majesty, are continually led into mistakes in the utterance of them, thereby often giving great offence to their owners, and exposing themselves unto derision and ridicule, to their no small discomfort and discomposure of mind; and moreover whereas a great many other inconveniences are by the same means occasioned;
>
> Be It Enacted, That from the passing of this Act, henceforth and for ever, no Person calling himself Chumley shall spell his name Cholmondely; and that all manner of Persons to think proper to spell their names Cholmondely, shall pronounce their said names, and have them pronounced of others, precisely as they

are spelt; that is to say, as words of four syllables, with a due and distinct emphasis on each.

And whereas the name of Beauchamp is of French origin, be at further enacted, that the said name shall be sounded of all men as nearly as possible after the French manner, and shall not be pronounced Beecham under any pretence whatever; and that all manner of Persons calling themselves Beecham shall write and spell their names, and shall have them written and spelt accordingly; provided always, that in case they prefer to spell them Beechum, they shall be at liberty so to do.

In like manner, Be it Further Enacted, That Marjoribanks shall be spelt Marchbanks; Wemys, Wims; and Colquhoun, Cohoun; or if not, then that they also shall be pronounced as they are spelt, and not in any other manner.

The penalty was severe. For each offence, five shillings. (That would be around £20 today.)

For other ***Punch*** **proposals**, see pp. 44, 93, 198.

Spoken and sungen

THE *past participle* is the form of a verb in such constructions as *I've* *walked* and *they're* *loved*. The *-ed* ending is the commonest one in modern English, and when a new verb comes along, it's usually given that ending, as in *I've emailed her*. But, in Old English, participles ending in *-en* were very common, and many of these have come down to us today. They're usually grouped along with other forms (such as *seen*) as 'irregular verbs', but that's not the best description when we think just how many of them there are – *broken*, *chosen*, *driven*, *eaten*, *fallen*, *forgotten*, *frozen*, *given*, *hidden*, *mistaken*, *risen*, *shaken*, *spoken*, *stolen*, *taken*, *trodden*, *woken*, *written* ... And there are verbal echoes in several adjectives, such as *drunken*, *grief-stricken*, *molten*, *shrunken*, *sunken* ...

'Irregular' is even less apposite when regional dialects are taken into account. Here are some from various places in the north of England, with their source verbs in parentheses:

bledden (bleed)
cutten (cut)
drovven (drive)
drucken (drink)
grutten (greet)
hitten (hit)
hodden (hold)
keppen (keep)
letten (let)
putten (put)
setten (set)
sprungen (spring)
stooden (stand)
strodden (stride)
stucken (stick)
throssen (thrust)

There are dozens more, and probably all regional dialects in England have some of them, even today. I still find myself sometimes saying *etten* (eaten) from the time when I lived in the north.

Several others can be found in earlier centuries, such as *holpen* (help) – and still used, according to Elizabeth Wright in her *Rustic Speech and Folklore* (1912), in Cheshire, Shropshire, and Rutland. But it could be anywhere. One never knows where such forms are going to turn up next, even in standard English. When people sing the Christmas carol 'Ding Dong Merrily on High' they use two of them without a second thought:

> Let steeple bells be swungen
> ... by priest and people sungen

Grammar and *Glamour*

THIS is my favourite example of a pair of words that don't obviously belong together, when in fact they share an etymological origin. *Glamour* was actually a Scots adaptation of *grammar*, relating to *gramarye*, in the sense of 'occult learning'. There was evidently something magical and mysterious about grammar – as I believe there still is, which is why I gave this subtitle to one of my books: 'The Glamorous Story of English Grammar'. But there are many others:

asterisk and *disaster*	common element 'star', from Latin *asteriscus* and earlier Greek 'little star'; Italian *dis* + *astro* 'ill-starred'
dentist and *dandelion*	common element 'tooth', from French and earlier Latin *dens*; French *dent de lion* 'lion's tooth', describing a plant whose leaves have a toothed outline
salary and *sausage*	common element 'salt', from Latin *salarium* 'money paid to soldiers to buy salt; Latin *salsus* 'salted [meat]'
lettuce and *galaxy*	common element 'milk', from Latin *lac* 'milk', here describing the milky appearance of the juice from the plant; earlier Greek *galaxias kuklos* 'milky circle' (as in the Milky Way)

Proverbial wisdom - 4

MORE proverbs translated into English from around the world, from my *As They Say in Zanzibar* (2006). This group is all to do with conversation.

Conversation is a ladder for a journey. [Sri Lanka]
A good conversation is better than a good bed. [Ethiopia]
After three days without reading, talk becomes flavourless. [China]
Gossip needs no carriage. [Russia]
That which is said at table should be wrapped up in the tablecloth. [Italy]
The story is only half told when one side tells it. [Iceland]
It may be true what some say; it must be true what all say. [Scotland]
Lovers have much to relate, but it is always the same thing. [Germany]
Those who gossip about their relatives have no luck and no blessing. [Netherlands]
Too much discussion will lead to a row. [Côte d'Ivoire]

And from England:

Least said, soonest mended.

For other examples of **proverbial wisdom**, see pp. 12, 51, 104, 182.

Lingua prancas – 3

MORE contributions to my blog challenge, where one has to choose a well-known expression in a foreign language, change or add a single letter, and provide a definition for the new expression. Sometimes a phrase elicited several alternatives:

a cappella

a cappellad	The choirboy sang on his own, because the organist was off sick.
a cappellag	One of the unaccompanied singers came in late.
a clappella	I was the only one who applauded.

magnum opus

magnum opud	The dessert was too big.
magnum opuss	I think I feed this cat too much.

sine qua non

sine qua none	I'm perfectly happy with my own company.
sine qua nun	Is that sister doing something she needs to confess?
sine quad non	You can't borrow my four-wheeled bike.
sink qua non	You can remove all the furniture but leave the kitchen alone.
cine qua non	No video filming allowed!

Other **lingua prancas** on pp. 25, 105.

Alliterative authorship

ANOTHER early Victorian obsession: alphabetical alliteration. The piece is called 'Title-page for a book of extracts from many authors'. The X cheat is ingenious.

Astonishing Anthology for Attractive Authors.
Broken Bits from Bulky Brains.
Choice Chunks from Chaucer to Channing.
Dainty Devices from Diverse Directions.
Echoes of Eloquence from Eminent Essayists.
Fragrant Flowers from Fields of Fancy.
Gems of Genius Gloriously Garnished.
Handy Helps from Head and Heart.
Illustrious Intellects Intelligently Interpreted.
Jewels of Judgment and Jets of Jocularity.
Kindlings to Keep from the King to the Kitchen.
Loosened Leaves from Literary Laurels.
Magnificent Morsels from Mighty Minds.
Numerous Nuggets from Notable Noodles.
Oracular Opinions Officiously Offered.
Prodigious Points from Powerful Pens.
Quirks and Quibbles from Queer Quarters.
Rare Remarks Ridiculously Repeated.
Suggestive Squibs from Sundry Sources.
Tremendous Thoughts on Thunderous Topics.

Utterances from Uppermost for Use and Unction.
Valuable View in Various Voices.
Wisps of Wit in a Wilderness of Words.
Xcellent Xtracts Xactly Xpressed.
Yawnings and Yearnings for Youthful Yankees.
Zeal and Zest from Zoroaster to Zimmerman.

Wanted

THIS advertisement appeared in the London *Times* in 1842:

> TO WIDOWERS AND SINGLE GENTLEMEN.–
> WANTED by a lady, a SITUATION to superintend the household and preside at table. She is Agreeable, Becoming, Careful, Desirable, English, Facetious, Generous, Honest, Industrious, Judicious, Keen, Lively, Merry, Natty, Obedient, Philosophic, Quiet, Regular, Sociable, Tasteful, Useful, Vivacious, Womanish, Xantippish, Youthful, Zealous, &c.

Quiet *and* vivacious? The alphabet has led her in some strange directions, especially at *X*. Xanthippe was the wife of Socrates. She must have thought this suggested wisdom. In fact, this name in English has always referred to an ill-tempered woman – a scold. If the ad was serious, it was likely to be successful only if an employer wasn't well read in Classical literature.

Lockdown 5 – Corona ...

THE term *coronavirus* equalled *COVID* for neologisms:

coronababy	a new human conceived during lockdown; also called a *coronial*; a member of what will be called *Generation C*
corona bonus	an unexpected benefit from having to stay at home or while out shopping
coronacoaster	ups and downs of mood during a typical lockdown day
coronacut	the usually unfortunate result of self-hair-dressing during self-isolation
coronadance	dancing in the street while maintaining social distancing
corona donor	someone you would not want to meet
coronalert	what we all have to be
coronaliterature	any creative writing about life during the crisis – including listings like this one; also called *coronalit*, along with its genres – *coronapoem*, *coronanovel*, etc.
corona loaner	anyone prepared to lend anything to help people get through the crisis
corona loner	someone who avoids all possible social contact when out taking exercise

corona moaner	someone who can't talk about anything else; also *corona groaner*
coronanoia	an irrational fear that the virus is all around us or is being passed on by the objects we see around us, such as radio masts; also *coronoia*
coronaphobia	a fear of coming into contact with the virus, especially as lockdown eases
corona phoner	someone who unnecessarily telephones everyone they know to check on their state of health
coronapocalypse and *coronageddon*	any interpretation of the virus as the end of the world
coronarhoea	a side-effect of the coronavirus
coronarita	a Margarita type of drink consumed during lockdown
coronasphere	the whole world
coronaspiracy	the view that a company or country – or any group of people – is hiding the truth about the origins or spread of the virus
coronasplainers	people who think they know more about the virus than anyone else; their behaviour is *coronasplaining*
coronavacation or *coronacation*	an enforced holiday from work as a result of having to stay at home
coronaverse	the whole world, and possibly other places to which the virus may already boldly have gone; also, poetry written while in isolation

coronavicar	a church minister who maintains online services during lockdown; similarly, there are *coronapriests*, *coronabishops*, and even a *coronapope*
coronawash	washing of the hands after imagining they might have been in contact with the virus
corooning	singing to others online or in the street

For other **lockdown** coinages,
see pp. 40, 54, 87, 121, 199.

How old?

When Mr. Bilbo Baggins announced that he would shortly be celebrating his eleventy-first birthday with a party of special magnificence, there was much talk and excitement in Hobbiton.

THE opening sentence of J R R Tolkien's *The Lord of the Rings* – linguistically interesting, for *eleventy* is more than just a joke-coinage. It's the first instance of the ancient ways of talking that are a major feature of the story. To see this, we need to know the Anglo-Saxon way of counting:

an [ahn], *twegen* [tway-uhn], *þri* [three] ...
then for the tens [with the final *-g* pronounced like the *y* of *you*] up to *fiftig* (50), *siextig* (60) ...
then with a *hund* prefix, *hundseofontig* (70), *hundeahtatig* (80), *hundnigontig* (90), *hundteontig* (100, also shorted to *hund* and *hundred*).

The reason for the addition of the prefix isn't known, but if we remove it, and modernize, we get *seventy*, *eighty*, *ninety*, *tenty* – and so *eleventy* (110) and *twelvety* (120). And Bilbo is *eleventy-one* – 111.

Having a system that counts up to 12 may seem alien, until we recall that it's still used in some measuring systems (as in 12 months, 24 hours), and in the notions of a *dozen* and a *gross*

(= 144 = 12 × 12). And this explains how Bilbo decided to limit the numbers invited to his party:

The invitations were limited to 12 dozen (a number also called by the hobbits one Gross, though the word was not considered proper to use of people).

Eating words

IN the third issue of *Verbatim* in 1983, Richard Lederer (p. 119) pulls together another amazing collection of metaphors – this time food-related. He begins:

> Now it is time to nibble on another spicy, meaty, juicy topic: the veritable banquet of mushrooming food metaphors that grace the table of our language and season our tongue. As we chew the fat about the food-filled expressions that are packed like sardines and sandwiched into our everyday conversation, you'll have a meal ticket to a cornucopia of food for thought.

Here's a further flavour:

> I have heard through the grapevine that you don't give a fig because you think that I'm out to lunch and nutty as a fruitcake; that you're giving me the raspberry for asking you to swallow a corny, mushy, soupy, cheesy, seedy, syrupy, sugar-coated, saccharine topic that just isn't your cup of tea, that you're beet red with anger at the idea of a pot-boiler that's no more than a tempest in a teapot; and that you're simmering because I'm out to cook your goose and egg you on by rehashing an old chestnut that's just pie in the sky and won't amount to a hill of beans.

But nuts to all that. You may think that my gastronomic metaphors are garbage, tripe, and a lot of baloney, but I plan to bring home the bacon, without hamming it up. The fruitful topic is no lemon. It's a plum.

And he goes on for another hundred or so before concluding:

In a nutshell, you now can see how often we try eat our words.

For more **Lederer**, see p. 119, and also his latest book, *A Feast of Words* (2023).

Dickens' linguistic portraits – 4

MRS General in *Little Dorrit* (1857), on having heard Amy address Mr Dorrit as 'Father':

> Papa is a preferable mode of address. Father is rather vulgar, my dear. The word Papa, besides, gives a pretty form to the lips. Papa, potatoes, poultry, prunes, and prism are all very good words for the lips: especially prunes and prism. You will find it serviceable, in the formation of a demeanour, if you sometimes say to yourself in company – on entering a room, for instance – Papa, potatoes, poultry, prunes and prism, prunes and prism.

Other **linguistic portraits** on pp. 29, 62, 106, 186.

Usage – 3

SOMETIMES a speaker starts off using a construction that requires a certain kind of follow-up, but gets into a tangle – such as here, from a nursing trainee:

> I've been stood by an incubator with a baby and explained it to.

He opens with an uncommon passive construction with *stand*, and then gets into trouble. He's clearly thinking 'and someone explained it to me', but the passive form is in his head, so he finds himself wanting to use it, and say 'and had it explained to me', but the processing goes wrong. It's another example of a syntactic blend (p. 123). Still, his listener had no trouble understanding what he meant.

For other **usage** issues, see pp. 47, 123, 195.

A Victorian univocalic - *U*

THESE are the most difficult to contrive, as there are far fewer words in English containing only *U*, compared to the others. This sequence follows on from 'Incontrovertible Facts' (p. 120):

> Dull humdrum murmurs lull, but hubbub stuns.
> Lucullus snuffs musk, mundungus[1] shuns.
> Puss purrs, buds burst, bucks butt, luck turns up
> trumps;
> But full cups, hurtful, spur up unjust thumps.

1 *Mundungus* was poor-quality, smelly tobacco. The word came into English in the 17th century, probably a borrowing from Spanish.

Fortunately, English has quite a few words that allow colloquial compositions, too. The task becomes easier if Y is allowed in, as in this example of 'A dog-show disagreement':

> Crufts furry puppy. Hush! Run, mutt, run, turn!
> Strut much stuff, fully push up stunts!
> Hurry, gutsy pug puppy!
> Gulp! Fluky jump. Lucky! Crumbs!
> Thumbs up? Cup?
> Ugh! Shucks! Humbug!
> Murmurs: fuddy-duddy dumb judgy churl unjust.

SCHMUCK!
Grunts: guru hunch sucks! Nuts! Bunkum! ****[1]
Glum. Mustn't blub. ...
Just drunk much rum. ...
Such fun. (Burp)

---

1 Here, an expletive was deleted.

For other **univocalics**, see pp. 2, 38, 80, 120.

Pickles on accents

WILFRED Pickles' experience as a BBC newsreader during World War II (p. 148) led him to worry about the way the classic BBC accent might eventually 'teach Great Britain to talk standard English'. He writes vividly in his autobiography:

> How terrible it is to think that we may some day lose that lovely soft Devonshire accent of the bluff and very wonderful Scots brogue or the amusing flatness and forthrightness of the North-countryman's speech, or the music of the Welsh voice. May it be forbidden that we should ever speak like B.B.C. announcers, for our rich contrast of voices is a vocal tapestry of great beauty and incalculable value, handed down to us by our forefathers. Our dialects are reminders of the permanence of things in these islands of ours, where folks talk differently in places only five miles apart, a phenomenon that has its roots in the times when it took many days to ride from London to York by stage coach.

He died in 1978, a year after the publication of the Annan Committee's report on the future of broadcasting, which included a recommendation that the BBC should present a wider range of accents.

Me, myself, and I

PROVERBS, being general truths, are usually expressed in an impersonal way, and in the present tense. But there are a few exceptions. Of over 2,000 proverbs from around the world collected in my *As They Say in Zanzibar* (2006), only 16 use the first person:

If I keep a green bough in my heart, a singing-bird will come. [China]
'If I rest, I rust,' says the key. [Germany]
God does not shave – why should I? [Bulgaria]
I can tell by my own pot how the others are boiling. [France]
The fish said, 'I have much to say, but my mouth is full of water.' [Georgia]
Ideas start with 'I'. [USA]
Who teaches me for a day is my father for a lifetime. [China]
Those who cheat me once, shame fall them; those who cheat me twice, shame fall me. [Scotland]
Their mosquito won't bite me. [Côte d'Ivoire]
The friends of my friends are my friends. [Belgium]
Your liberty ends where my nose begins. [USA]
The enemies of my enemies are my friends. [France]
My banjo has no bells on it. [Nigeria]
I gave an order to a cat, and the cat gave it to its tail. [China]
If my aunt had wheels, she might be an omnibus. [Netherlands]
If you don't like my apples, don't shake my tree. [USA]

I don't get it – 2

Death is nothing new for TV,
but Six Feet Under has refreshed the parts other biers cannot reach.

THIS was the heading of a British newspaper television review article in 2005. But how many English speakers in the world would get the allusion? Only those who were around when Heineken started its long-running lager slogan in 1974: *Heineken refreshes the parts other beers cannot reach.* It became a catchphrase in the UK because the ad campaign used it there, in various forms, for over 20 years. In countries where that campaign didn't run, such as the USA, people are unlikely to get the joke.

For another example of **I don't get it**, see p. 50.

Descriptions – 3

GERALD Durrell, of Ursula Pendragon's grim, determined, unremitting battle with the English language, in *Fillets of Plaice* (1971, Chapter 6):

> Where other people meekly speak their mother tongue in the way that it is taught them, Ursula adopted a more militant and Boadicea-like approach. She seized the English language by the scruff of the neck, shook it thoroughly, turned it inside out, and forced words and phrases to do her bidding, making them express things they were never meant to express.

For more **descriptions**, see pp. 97, 128.

Going global - 4

TRISTAN da Cunha is a tiny island archipelago in the middle of the South Atlantic. It was named after the Portuguese admiral who discovered it in 1506. First settled in 1816, it became a British dependency in 1938. The original settlers were seamen from London, Devon, Scotland, and Cape Town, along with later American whalers, and their speech left its mark on the local dialect.

Its isolation and small size – the population grew to only a couple of hundred – gave it a unique linguistic character. In vocabulary, its seafaring origins is reflected, for example, in the way the community refers to itself as *all hands*. A cattle enclosure is a *kraal* (from Afrikaans). A knitted pullover is a *gansey* ('Guernsey', known in Scotland and Ireland). *Gulch* and *bluff* are American.

Here are a dozen examples of the local lexicon, from Arne Zettersten's *The English of Tristan da Cunha* (1969):

Kettle	a saucepan
Train	a cart
pot-of-all-kinds	a fruit salad
jacket	a blouse
blow-up	a young man
fardie	a godfather
madish	a godmother

to be sergeants	to be good friends
diceling	a dock plant
prickle-bush	gorse
egg shirt	a loose overshirt in which penguin eggs are collected
bosom of eggs	the egg shirt when filled

Tristan da Cunha became world-famous in 1961, when its volcano erupted, forcing the entire population to be evacuated. They lived in England for 18 months, before deciding to return. And while there, linguists at University College London under Randolph Quirk took the opportunity to record their speech – which is why we know so much about their dialect.

For more **Going global**, see pp. 52, 103, 143, 194.
For the most unusual linguistic feature of Tristan da Cunha, see p. 206.

Comic alphabets – 4

THE most familiar examples today, usually beginning 'A for 'orses', can be traced back to the early years of the 20th century, with many variations. The most famous of all the first creations was the one compiled by the music-hall comedy double act of Charlie Clapham (1894–1959) and Bill Dwyer (1887–1943), who first broadcast it on radio in 1929 (one of many early recordings destroyed during the London Blitz in World War II). A version of their 'surrealist alphabet' appeared in the *Daily Express* in 1936, shown here with Eric Partridge's emendations reflecting what he thought was the original. There were many later variations, including some set to music for dance bands, such as 'The New Swing Alphabet' recorded by Jack Jackson and His Band in 1937. (I add glosses for people unfamiliar with the slang and culture of the time.)

A for 'orses [hay for horses, with *h* dropped in the Cockney accent]
B for mutton [beef or mutton]
C for thighlanders [Seaforth Highlanders – a British army regiment]
D for dumb [deaf or dumb]
E for brick [heave a brick – lifting something heavy]
F fervescence [effervescence]
G for police [chief of police]
H for retirement [age]
I falutin [high falutin – pretentiously fancy]

J affa oranges [from the city of Jaffa, now part of Tel Aviv]
K ferancis [Kay Francis][1]
L for leather [hell for leather – as fast as possible]
M phasis [emphasis]
N for a penny [in for a penny][2]
O ver the garden wall[3]
P for a penny [it cost a penny to enter a public toilet]
Q for seats [queue for seats]
R for mo [half a mo(ment) – a short time, with *h* dropped in the Cockney accent]
S for you [as for you]
T for two [tea for two – a popular song of the 1920s]
U ferinstance [you, for instance]
V for la France [Vive la France – long live France]
W for a bob [double you for a shilling – raising the bet in a game]
X for breakfast [eggs ...]
Y for heaven's sake [why ...]
Z furbreezes [zephyr breezes][4]

1 One of the best-known American film actresses of the 1930s – aged 31 in 1936.

2 The first part of the proverb 'In for a penny, in for a pound', meaning 'if you start something, carry it through'.

3 A Victorian music-hall song, the point being that it's all about a romance between lovers in adjacent gardens, an irate father, and an elopement.

4 From the Greek name of the god of the west wind, Zephyros. It's the least successful of the entries, as it requires a semi-American pronunciation to work – zee, rather than zed. In later British versions, usually replaced by a line where Z = 'said'.

For other **comic alphabets**, see pp. 9, 64, 135, 202.

Collecting collectives – 5

A LAST group of possibilities for collective nouns:

a quake of seismologists
a ring of keys
a scarcity of ghosts
a scattering of kittens
a sea of bishops
a snap of photographers
a stack of librarians
an assessment of examiners
an assortment of fonts
an audit of accountants
an illusion of magicians
an intrusion of spammers

Other **collectives** on pp. 3, 32, 66, 133.

Proverbial wisdom – 5

MORE proverbs translated into English from around the world, from my *As They Say in Zanzibar* (2006, p. 12). This group is all to do with reading and writing.

The wise read a letter backwards. [Germany]
By writing we learn to write. [France]
Good scribes are not those who write well, but who erase well. [Russia]
Those who can read and write have four eyes. [Albania]
Never argue with someone who buys ink by the barrel. [China]
One can study calligraphy at eighty. [Japan]
What one writes remains. [Netherlands]
Wise silence has never been written down. [Italy]
When in anger, say the alphabet. [USA]
Life without literature is death. [Latin]

And from England:

The heart's letter is read in the eye.

For other examples of **proverbial wisdom**, see pp. 12, 51, 104, 156.

Not so long ago

WHEN we read something written at the beginning of the 19th century, the language seems very close to what we use today – identical, at times. But if we heard it spoken, we'd get a very different impression. Here are some of the words from the first two letters of the alphabet, as reported by John Walker in his *English Pronouncing Dictionary* (1891), where the pronunciation noticeably differs from the one we hear today.

Different stress

Now	*Then*
abdomen	abdomen
acceptable	acceptable
acumen	acumen
balcony	balcony
barricade	barricade
blackguard	blackguard

Vowels

	Now	*Then*
aerial	*ae* as in *air*	*a* and *e* kept separate
amenity	*e* as in *me*	*e* as in *met*
armada	second *a* as in *ah*	second *a* as in *may*
beauty	byou-tee	boo-tee
borough	*ou* as in unstressed *the*	*ou* as in *no*
Brazil	*il* as in *ill*	*il* as in *eel*

Consonants

	Now	*Then*
annihilate	*h* not pronounced	*h* pronounced
anxiety	*anx* as *angz*	*anx* as *anks*
axiom	akseeum	akshum
brick-kiln	*n* pronounced	*n* not pronounced
bristle	*t* not pronounced	*t* pronounced
brothel	*th* as in *thin*	*th* as in *this*

Tom Brown 3 – on boring books

IN 1691, satirist Tom Brown wrote a dialogue called 'Wit for Money', which includes a dig at his own profession.

JOHNSON: Let's go to the Booksellers, and see what new Books are sprung up since last Night.

SMITH: With all my heart: but methinks thou mak'st Mushrooms of them: If some Reverend Author, or Waspish Satyrist heard thee, thou wou'd be in danger of a lash in his next Weeks Pamphlet.

JOHNSON: Authors and Satyrists do you call them? Scribblers, Libellers, and Lampooners, are more suitable Epithets for many of them; and for my part, I oftner take up their Papers to pick out their Nonsense, and laugh at it, than to find any thing worthy observation.

SMITH: Oh, I have found out another use for them; formerly I cou'd not sleep, tho I desired it; but having bought a Book call'd The Moralist, I began to read it one Night, having no other by my Bed side, when even Opium cou'd not purchase me sleep, and before I had read two Pages, I slept so fast, that I found the next Morning my Candle in the Socket, and the Book in the Chamber-pot.

JOHNSON: And a very fit place for it, and all such dull, insipid, heavy, unweildy[1] sustain.

---

1 This isn't a typo, just an early spelling.

For more **Tom Brown**, see pp. 27, 85, 208.

Dickens' linguistic portraits – 5

Mr Meagles in *Little Dorrit* (1857):

NARRATOR: Never by any accident acquired any knowledge whatever of the language of any country in which he travelled.

MEAGLES: Anything short of speaking the language I shall be delighted to undertake.

NARRATOR: With an unspoken confidence that the English tongue was somehow the mother tongue of the whole world, only the people were too stupid to know it, Mr Meagles harangued innkeepers in the most voluble manner, entered into loud explanations of the most complicated sort, and utterly renounced replies in the native language of the respondents, on the ground that they were

MEAGLES: All bosh.

Other **linguistic portraits** on pp. 29, 62, 106, 169.

Swingin' the alphabet

THE alphabet has often been the source of songs, especially for little children, but there are adult versions, too. Probably the most famous is the one sung by the Three Stooges in the 1938 film *Violent is the Word for Curly* – a version of a song originally written by Septimus Winner in 1875. Larry, Moe, and Curly have ended up (thanks to various plot twists, far too complicated to summarise here) dressed as professors at Mildew College in front of a class of young women.

They sing the consonants with vowels attached, pointing to the letters on a blackboard: 'B A bay- B E bee – B I biki by – B O bo biki by boh – B U boo – biki-by-boh – boo'. The lyrics – if that's the right word – are the same for each letter apart from the first syllable: 'C A say, C E see', and so on. At D the class joins in, close harmonising, and they get to M before they take a bow. It's all viewable on YouTube.

Wright's words – 4

A SELECTION of speech-related words from Joseph Wright's *English Dialect Dictionary* (p. 8):

beflum [*verb*] Known in Yorkshire and Scotland.
Deceive by using cajoling language. 'I couldn't have been more beflummed if I'd been a lawyer.' *Flum* is from *flummox*, which started life as a dialect word.

buzznacking [*noun and verb*] Known in Cumbria, Devon, Somerset, Yorkshire.
Fussing, gossipng – a blend of *buzz* and *knack*, 'chatter'. But *knack* also meant 'talk in an affected way', so we see sentences from Yorkshire like 'She knacks like a London miss.'

doggery-baw [*noun*] Known in Lincolnshire.
Nonsense. 'He talks such doggery-baw.' To 'speak doggery' goes back at least to the 16th century. It meant 'be rude or insulting'.

jawbation [*noun*] Widespread across the eastern and southern Midlands, and the southern counties from Sussex to Somerset.
A long and tedious harangue, especially a scolding or reprimand. 'He drove me crazy with his jawbation.' And in some places, such as Yorkshire, you'd be described as *jawbacious.*

mattery [*adjective*] Known in Northumberland.
Wordy, loquacious. Said especially of someone when they're making a fuss. 'He's a mattery old fella.' This is *matter* in the sense of 'content'.

wordify [*verb*] Known in Devon and Yorkshire.
To put into words. 'It's no use you goin' on wordifying when there's a job to be done.' It's the sort of thing a lot of people do in this book selection. Its opposite is *wordshy*.

For other words from
The Disappearing Dictionary, see pp. 81, 134.

Word Ways remembered - 3

In 1981, the magazine published several examples of what it called 'alphabetic recitals', where a story is told reflecting the sounds of the letter-names. The genre ideally uses only words that are homonymic with the names, but near-homonyms are inevitable. There's no insistence on the text making complete sense, thank goodness! Here's a British example, from Allan Simmons:

Eh! Be seedy, ye effigy, at shy Jake
A lemon, opaque. You are a stew -
Feed a bull, you ex! Why said?

That ending wouldn't work in American English, as this other example from the time, by Boris Randolph, illustrates.

Abie see de eel elf. Gee! Etch high Jake.
Hey! Element toe pique you? Arrest tea. You've eel.
Double you eggs. Why zeal?

For other ***Word Ways* remembered**, see pp. 45, 113.

Another Shakespearean find

THE extraordinary interest raised by the discovery of the H Quarto (p. 73) led the organisers of the annual meeting of the International Association of Teachers of English as a Foreign Language (IATEFL) in 2010 to ask if there had been any further discoveries. Fortunately, the finding of a fragment of the rumoured M Quarto of *Macbeth* allowed a presentation of Macbeth's famous speech in Act 2 Scene 1, shown here with the official lines as glosses.

[Is this a dagger which I see before me?]
Machete materialising?
[The handle toward my hand? Come, let me clutch thee.]
Midpoint marking my mitt? Move, must manipulate.
[I have thee not, and yet I see thee still.]
Missed! Meanwhile mirage maintains mien.
[Art thou not, fatal vision, sensible]
Maybe, mortiferous manifestation, making malleable
[To feeling as to sight? Or art thou but]
My muscles, massaging my myopia? Maybe
[A dagger of the mind, a false creation,]
Mental machete, misapprehension, mistake,
[Proceeding from the heat-oppressed brain?]
Molten medulla manifesting mental mirage.
[I see thee yet, in form as palpable]
Mirage manifesting material manner

[As this which now I draw.]
Mirroring mine mobilising.
[Thou marshall'st me the way that I was going;]
Marshall'st me, motivating my movements,
[And such an instrument I was to use]
Modelling my mechanism method.
[Mine eyes are made the fools o' the other senses,]
Manifold motor-messages muddled my myopia
[Or else worth all the rest; I see thee still,]
Maybe my myopia more meritable; mirage maintains
[And on thy blade and dudgeon gouts of blood,]
Machete members manifest myriad metarteriole
mega-mounds
[Which was not so before. There's no such thing:]
Missing meanwhile. Mighty misconception!
[It is the bloody business which informs]
My metarteriolic mission must message
[Thus to mine eyes. Now o'er the one halfworld]
Much mine myopia. Meantime midst mini-planet
moiety
[Nature seems dead, and wicked dreams abuse]
Macrocosm maybe morgued, malignant musings
molest
[The curtain'd sleep; witchcraft celebrates]
Montage-masked Morpheus-mode; magic-maids make
merry
[Pale Hecate's offerings, and wither'd murder,]
Mini-hued major-magic-maid's munificence; mouldy
murder
Alarum'd by his sentinel, the wolf,]
Made mindful, malicious mammal monitored,

[Whose howl's his watch, thus with his stealthy pace,]
Moan-monitoring, making mute measure,
[With Tarquin's ravishing strides, towards his design]
Mirroring maiden-molester's moves, match-meeting motive
[Moves like a ghost. Thou sure and firm-set earth,]
Moves mirage-like. Mightily massed marl
[Hear not my steps, which way they walk, for fear]
Mishear my movements; meandering motion might
[The very stones prate of my whereabout,]
Make masonry mention my map-reference
[And take the present horror from the time,]
Marooning monstrosity moment,
[Which now suits with it. Whiles I threat, he lives:]
Meanwhile matching. Menace-meditating, monarch maintains mettle
[Words to the heat of deeds too cold breath gives.]
Morphemes massively melt motions

Bell rings

[I go, and it is done; the bell invites me.]
Move momentarily, Macbeth, mission made; melody manoeuvres me.
[Hear it not, Duncan; for it is a knell]
Mishear, Monarch. Mayday music
[That summons thee to heaven or to hell.]
Maybe mooting marvellous merriment, maybe miserable moan.

Exit

Going global – 5

IN 1997, Bernard Share published *Slanguage – a Dictionary of Slang and Colloquial English* in Ireland. Here are some expressions from it:

I'm all behind like the cow's tail	I'm running very late
I didn't come up the river on a bike	I'm no fool
to have larks for breakfast/supper	to be extremely eloquent
put a tooth in it	get to the point
the same man with his knee bent	said of two very similar people, things, or events
you could trot a mouse across it	said of very strong tea

For more **Going global**, see pp. 52, 103, 143, 177.

Usage – 4

PEOPLE can get themselves into an awful tangle when they're thinking of actions taking place in the past. Here are three examples, all spoken perfectly naturally and unselfconsciously, without hesitation. But they are a pain to analyse.

> Mother won't want to go to the wedding tomorrow. In the old days it was different. She would used to have chosen to go.
> There's someone at the door. It's the man that you want to have come to see you.
> They must not be having developed a sense of responsibility.

For other **usage** issues, see pp. 47, 123, 170.

New proverbs

AMBROSE Bierce, in *The Devil's Dictionary* (p. 69), introduced a further dimension to proverb manipulation. This is his entry on *saw*:

> A trite popular saying, or proverb. So called because it makes its way into a wooden head. Following are examples of old saws fitted with new teeth.
> A penny saved is a penny to squander.
> A man is known by the company that he organizes.
> A bad workman quarrels with the man who calls him that.
> A bird in the hand is worth what it will bring.
> Better late than before anybody has invited you
> Example is better than following it.
> Half a loaf is better than a whole one if there is much else.
> Think twice before you speak to a friend in need.
> What is worth doing is worth the trouble of asking somebody to do it.
> Least said is soonest disavowed.
> He laughs best who laughs least.
> Speak of the Devil and he will hear about it.
> Of two evils choose to be the least.
> Strike while your employer has a big contract.
> Where there's a will there's a won't.

For more **Ambrose Bierce**, see pp. 71, 145.

Being – 3

A WHOLE new set of forms express what in standard English since the 18th century appears as *aren't/are not*. In Old and Middle English we see *nart*, *n'art*, and *nert* – in early Middle English sometimes with the pronoun attached: *nartu*, *nertu*. The variations grow after the 16th century: *arn't*, *are'nt*, *ar'n't*, *an't*, in Scotland *arnae* and *arna*, and everywhere *ain't*. Some dialects use forms based on *art*: *artn't*, *artna*, and the unusual-looking *atten*. There are some fascinating combinations, such as this one from Tennessee in 1827: 'Thou an't sick, child, art thee?'

Also, during the 16th century, we see forms recorded based on *be*. Some simply add the negative particle (in various pronunciations), as in *bent*, *bain't*, *binna*, *byant*, *beant*. Some add it to *bist* or *be's*, with apostrophes scattered throughout: *beesnt*, *beestna*, *bisnt*, *bistnt*, *bis'n't*, *be s'n't*. From the 18th century and after, there are recorded forms based on *is*: *you isn't*, *i't*, *in't*.

But the crowning glory of all the distinctive forms for the second person has surely got to be what happened in the 19th century to *ain't* followed by a pronoun. The fashion in representing colloquial speech was to show the assimilation of the final consonant of *ain't* and the initial consonant of *you*, resulting in *aintcha*. It was spelled in all sorts of ways: as well as *aintcha* we find *aincha*, *ain'tcha*, *ain't'cha*, *ain't-cha*, and *aint'cha*. *Aren't you* received the same treatment: *aren'cha*, *arencha*, *arentcha*, *aren'tcha*. *Ain'tcha* became famous because it proved to be a particular favourite of singers, such as Frank Sinatra ('Ain'tcha ever coming back') and Simon and Garfunkel ('Ain'tcha got no rhymes for me?').

For other examples of ***be* variation**, see pp 41, 107.

Proposals from *Punch* - 4

MR Punch was evidently impressed by this proposal, reported in Volume 22 (1852):

> Somebody has started, what may be called, with reference to the Alphabet, a CAPITAL idea, by proposing to teach children their letters through the medium of Lozenges. Instead of appealing to the eye, the inventor appeals to the mouth, and thus the sweets of learning are made – not simply a name, but a luscious reality.
>
> In these days, when premature cramming is so common, it is something to invent a plan for causing instruction to go down agreeably. A thirst for knowledge is an excellent thing, but the Alphabet Lozenges will encourage not only an absolute hunger, but a right-down greediness for learning.
>
> Some may doubt the propriety of blending instruction with the lollipop, and allowing the influence of the cane to be superseded by that of the sugar-stick. We think that a wholesome effect might be produced by conveying information into a medical form, and we throw out the hint for combining salubrity with science, by the invention of a multiplication pill, a geographical black dose, and an ointment to be rubbed in for the purpose of rubbing up a knowledge of history.

For other ***Punch* proposals**, see pp. 44, 93, 151.

Lockdown 6 – a miscellany

A last memory of the COVID neologistic era.

BC	Before Covid *or* Before Coronavirus; also *BCV*
BCE	Before the Covid Era *or* Before the Coronavirus Era
drivecation	getting into one's parked car to gain the feeling of going on holiday
elbump	a gentle nudge used to avoid hand-shaking; now obsolete and possibly illegal when there is a 2-metre rule; also, *elbowshake*
infodemic	the spread of false news about the virus
isobar	a home stock of alcohol brought in to survive lockdown
isobath	taking a bath alone, or with fresh water, just in case
iso-breaker	a remark made at the beginning of an online conversation that makes everyone feel comfortable
isocooking	devising or sharing new home recipes during lockdown; also called *isobaking*
iso-creams	the possibility of cones, wafers, etc. fitted with an edible app that would warn you if you were getting too close to someone else eating them; also, *iso-lollies*

isodesking having a desk at work or at home that is at least 2 metres away from anyone else

iso-hockey a possible variant of the traditional game in which you are not allowed to come within 2 metres of any other player

isolocks the growth of hair resulting from the inability to go to a hairdresser

lickdown a ban on offering your ice-cream cone to others; see also *iso-creams*

lochdown a ban on visiting Scottish lakes

lockdowner anyone in a state of imposed isolation

locksit the way out of a period of lockdown; also *lexit* and *loxit*

locktail a cocktail created during a lockdown; usually drunk during a *locktail hour*

maskee or *masker* anyone wearing a protective face-mask

masklessee anyone refusing to wear a protective face-mask

miley rhyming slang for the virus, as in 'Have you 'ad the miley?' – from the singer Miley Cyrus

morona anyone behaving in an idiotic way – a *covidiot*

risolating experiencing an irrational desire to eat rice-pudding during lockdown

riso-pudding a failed attempt to create a new rice-based dessert during lockdown

ronavation	getting on with home improvements during lockdown
safewishing	the usual way of ending an online message; also, *safetywishing*
scamdemic	the spread of online fraudulent messages purporting to be from genuine sources
twiceolation	a second period of enforced quarantine
thriceolation	a third period of enforced quarantine
upperwear	the part of your clothing that can be seen on screen
viso-president	a politician who keeps a safe distance from the president
Y2K	short for *Y2Kovid* – the real start of the new millennium

For other **lockdown** coinages, see pp. 40, 54, 87, 121, 162.

Comic alphabets - 5

ALL the letters in this genre had many variants, as authors strove to be original. Eric Partridge made a collection of as many as he could find. The vowels attract the most creations, with O top with 14. In the first 11 cases, O fer = Over; in the last three, O = Oh!

O fer and over
O fer arm [overarm – bowling in cricket]
O fer board
O fer night
O fer the garden wall
O fer the hill [unable to do something because of old age]
O fer the rainbow [song in The Wizard of Oz, 1939]
O fer the top [war cry of soldiers attacking from a trench during World War I]
O fer there [popular 1917 American wartime song]
O fer to you
O fer we go
O for a beer/drink/etc.
O for goodness' sake
O for the wings of a dove/the open road/etc. – literary references

For other **comic alphabets**, see pp. 9, 64, 135, 179.

F*** is off

DICTIONARIES always have a 'running head' printed at the top corner of each page, as a means of helping readers find their way through the book. So, if the first entry on the left-hand page is *challenge*, the running head will be *challenge*; and if the last entry on the right-hand page is *chance*, the running head on that page will be *chance*. It is always the first entry on the left and the last entry on the right. Or rather, almost always. On one page of the 1981 edition of *The Macquarie Dictionary*, the editors encountered a problem. The running head shows *fuchsite*, which is actually the *penultimate* entry on the right-hand page. No prizes for guessing which word was the real last entry on that page.

Dickens' voice portraits – 5

THE land agent Mr Scadder in *Martin Chuzzlewit* (1844):

> He was a gaunt man in a huge straw hat, and a coat of green stuff. The weather being hot, he had no cravat, and wore his shirt collar wide open; so that every time he spoke something was seen to twitch and jerk up in his throat, like the little hammers in a harpsichord when the notes are struck. Perhaps it was the Truth feebly endeavouring to leap to his lips. If so, it never reached them.

Other **voice portraits** on pp. 6, 48, 84, 147.

How much, did you say? – 5

WHAT about the pound, in Shakespeare's day? Originally a pound weight of silver, it became a standard monetary unit of measurement used in accounting to express values and costs. Until 1583, it didn't exist as a coin (nor as a pound note, which was a much later development), but its value was represented by the gold sovereign, in use since the time of Henry VII, and in the later part of the century worth about 20 shillings (240 old pence). The pound evidently had strong psychological value, as everyone talks about it, from rich to poor.

At the top end of the scale, we learn in Act 3 of *Cymbeline* that a British tribute to Rome was £3,000 a year (£300,000 today). Among the wealthy, everyday pocket money seems to have been £100 or so. In Act 2 of the same play, Prince Cloten is prepared to bet £100 on a throw at bowls. That's quite a bet: £10K today.

At the other end of the scale, in Act 3 of *Henry IV Part 1* we see the Hostess trying to get some money out of Falstaff:

> You owe money here besides, Sir John, for your diet,
> and by-drinkings, and money lent you, four-and-twenty
> pound.

The costs have evidently built up – over £2K today. It sounds as if the Hostess has a cash-flow problem.

For other **How much ...?**, see pp. 10, 42, 92, 144.

Long, longer ...

VERY long place-names are unusual, so when they occur, they become the focus of (especially tourist) attraction. Most people in Britain are aware of the 58-letter name in Wales (hyphenated here for ease of reading):

> *Llan-fair-pwll-gwyn-gyll-goger-y-chwyrn-drobwll-llan-tysilio-gogo-goch*
> 'Church (of) Mary (in the) hollow (of the) white hazel near the rapid whirlpool (and) church of (saint) Tysilio (by the) red cave'

In the North Island of New Zealand, you will see road signs directing you to 'The Longest Place Name in the World', with 85 letters (again, hyphenated):

> *Taumata-whakatangi-hanga-koauau-o-Tamatea-turi-pukaka-piki-maunga-horo-nuku-pokai-whenua-kitana-tahu.*
> 'The hilltop where Tamatea, the man with the big knees, conqueror of mountains, eater of land, traveller over land and sea, played his kōauau to his beloved.'

A kōauau is a Māori flute. I tell the story of this encounter in the paperback edition of *By Hook or by Crook* (2007).

But Tristan da Cunha (p. 177) beats both, with its long descriptive names for local features, such as:

The-hill-with-a-hole-in-it
Where-Times-fell-off gulch – Times was the name of a dog
Down-where-the-minister-land-his-things – a beach name, where a clergyman landed during a storm in 1906
The-ridge-where the goat-jump-off

And so to this one, which (including the hyphens) is 103 letters:

The-hill-with-a-pond-in-it-on-the-east-side-of-the-gulch-come-down-by-the-ridge-where-the-goat-jump-off

English inn-names – 3

TOM Brown wrote vividly wicked descriptions of the life and times of 17th-century London. In number 10 of his *Amusements serious and comical*, he shows an imagined visitor from the Indies around the city, and encounters the puzzling world of inn-sign names.

> From the Gaming-House we took our Walk through the Streets, and the first Amusements we Encountred, were the Variety and contradictory Language of the *Signes*, enough to perswade a Man there were no Rules of Concord among the Citizens. Here we saw *Ioseph*'s *Dream*, the *Bull and Mouth*, the *Hen and Razor*, the *Ax and Bottle*, the *Whale and Crow*, the *Shovel and Boot*, the *Leg and Star*, the *Bible and Swan*, the *Frying-Pan and Drum*, the *Lute and Tun*, the *Hog Armour*, and a thousand others that the wise Men that put them there can give no Reason for.

For other **inn-names**, see pp. 37, 138.
For more **Tom Brown**, see pp. 27, 85, 185.

Telling the future, almost

THIS is an article from *The Daily Mirror*:

> English and French will become world languages if a post-war scheme discussed at a United Nations education conference in London is carried through.
>
> The scheme envisages a world-wide auxiliary language and a system of interchanges of students and teachers.
>
> One of the primary objects is an interchange of young people between nations which would foster understanding and international friendships and kindle social and cultural interests.
>
> The conference agreed that English should become the auxiliary language to be taught in primary schools, except in English-speaking countries, where French should be taught.

The date was 30 June 1943.

Making a living from non-standard English

ARTEMUS Ward was the pseudonym of American humourist Charles Farrer Browne (1834–67), who made himself famous, both in the USA and abroad, by his lectures, always delivered in a grave melancholy manner full of regional vocabulary and pronunciations, and written up in non-standard spelling. This short piece was called 'Experience as an Editor', and published in a collection of his essays in 1862.

> In the Ortum of 18– my frend, the editor of the Baldinsville Bugle, was obleged to leave perfeshernal dooties & go & dig his taters, & he axed me to edit for him doorin his absence. Accordinly I ground up his Shears and commenced. It didn't take me a grate while to slash out copy enuff from the xchanges for one issoo, and I thawt I'd ride up to the next town on a little Jaunt, to rest my Branes which had bin severely rackt by my mental efforts. (This is sorter Ironical.) So I went over to the Rale Rood offiss and axed the Sooprintendent for a pars.
>
> '*You* a editer?' he axed, evidently on the pint of snickering.
> 'Yes Sir,' sez I, 'don't I look poor enuff?'
> 'Just about,' sed he, 'but our Road can't pars you.'
> 'Can't, hey?'
> 'No Sir – it can't.'

'Becauz,' sez I, lookin him fall in the face with a Eagle eye '*it goes so durned slow it can't pars anybody*!' Methinks I had him thar. It's the slowest Rail Road in the West. With a mortifi'ed air, he told me to git out of his offiss. I pittid him and went.

It is perfect

IN 1855, a little book was published in Paris with the title *O novo guia da conversação em portuguez e inglez* (The new guide to conversation in Portuguese and English), compiled by Pedro Carolino and José da Fonseca. It became hugely popular because of the unintentional humour resulting from its many errors. It was reprinted in 1883 with the title *English as She is Spoke*, and the American edition had an introduction by Mark Twain, who gave it great praise: 'Its delicious unconscious ridiculousness, and its enchanting naïveté, are as supreme and unapproachable, in their way, as are Shakespeare's sublimities.' 'It is perfect' are his words. This example of Dialogue 40 illustrates its character:

> FOR TO SWIM.
> It is very warm.
> Go to row.
> I like better to see the swimmers what to row myself.
> Sir, do you row well?
> He swim as a fish.
> I swim on the cork. It is dangerous to row with bladders, because its put to break.
> I row upon the belly on the back and between two waters: I know also to plunge.
> I am not so dexterous that you.

> I do not what to begin. I am going to the swimming school.
> Nothing is more easy than to swim; it do not what don't to be afraid of.
> You go give me a lesson, and you will see that I know to do.
> Tel undress us.
> The water is excellent, it is too hot.
> It is more agreeable to bathe one's self in even water that in one baignoire.
> The weather it is cloudy it lighten. I think we go to have storm.
> Go out of the water quickly.

On the back of the 1883 edition the publisher advertises *English as She is Wrote*, and several other titles later appeared in the same burlesque style, such as *Britain as She is Visit* by Paul Jennings in 1976.

Astrolinguistics

IF you're inventing an alien race, you have to invent a language, too, and several now exist, such as Na'vi, the language of the humanoids who live on the moon Pandora, explored in the 2009 film *Avatar*. Na'vi joins a family of invented languages created to add linguistic verisimilitude to science fiction films.

But there are still quite a large number of aliens who evidently do speak English. The question is: what kind of English should they speak? If the beings look really alien, and behave in an alien way, then they should sound alien, too. On the other hand, one has to be practical. The accent mustn't be so different or difficult that it can't be easily pronounced by the characters or understood by the audience.

Friendly aliens usually have a standard English accent. They speak like us – therefore they like us. Enemy aliens follow the opposite principle: their voices are as far away as possible from normal English – though not so far that the speech will be unintelligible. The solutions keep the vowels and consonants fairly standard and manipulate the tone of voice, following the familiar principle of 'It ain't what you say but the way that you say it'. The following examples are from the book *You Say Potato: A Book about Accents* (2015) by David and Ben Crystal.

Faced with the task of devising a voice to make Daleks intelligible yet super-evil, the recipe is plain. Let them use normal vowels and consonants, so that they're understandable, but take away every feature of intonation and rhythm that reminds you of normal human English. Make them speak in a monotone with abnormal rising lilts. Add a staccato rhythm. Not 'exterminate' but 'ex-ter-min-ate', with each syllable prominent. Lengthen some vowels more than they would normally sound. Add a touch of haranguing loudness. And introduce a metallic voice quality that no human voice could possibly achieve.

Most enemy aliens using English have a deviant voice quality that affects the way they speak. They can sound hoarse, or nasal, or creaky, or breathy, or all of these together. Weird intonations and rhythms are commonplace. *Doctor Who*'s Cybermen, who have no emotions at all, compete with Daleks for monotone and staccato. Zygons speak in low-pitched, hissing, whispering voices. And altering an accent can have devastating effects. In 'The Robots of Death' (from the days when the Doctor was played by Tom Baker) the villain is destroyed by one of his own robots when the Doctor's assistant releases some helium gas, causing his voice to become high-pitched and squeaky. As a result he is no longer recognized by his robots, who turn on him and kill him. This may well be the only recorded case of an accent modification actually being fatal.

English Language Day

ALL languages should have their celebratory days. In the case of English, the United Nations in 2010 chose 23 April, for no other reason than that it coincided with Shakespeare's birthday. A rather more meaningful choice, reflecting the language as a whole, was made by The English Project – a Winchester-based group planning the first permanent English-language exhibition space in the country, to be located in that city. It chose 13 October, because on that day, in 1362, the Chancellor of England for the first time opened Parliament with a speech in English. In that same Parliament, a Statute of Pleading was approved that permitted members in debate to use the English language.

Why not take up some of the linguistic challenges from this miscellany on English Language Day?

Answers

Nashisms (p. 98)
I sit in an office at 244 Madison Avenue
And say to myself You have a reasonable job, havenue?

I would live all my life in nonchalance and insouciance
Were it not for making a living, which is rather a nouciance.

Have you ever gone visiting for a weekend of ravelry
Only to find yourself surrounded by the Cavalry?

He who attempts to tease the cobra
Is soon a sadder he, and sobra.

One thing that literature would be greatly the better for
Would be a more restricted employment by authors of simile and metaphor.

The folk who live in Scandinavia
Are famous for their odd behavia.

The ostrich roams the great Sahara.
Its mouth is wide, its neck is narra.

Word bluffing (p. 140)
Number 3 in each case.

Unfinished proverbs (p. 115)
There may be slight differences in phrasing.

... and you'll get a silly answer.
... the heart cannot grieve about.
... wear it.
... laugh longest.
... shouldn't throw stones.
... is in the eating.
... keeps the doctor away.
... make light work.
... I'll scratch yours.
... is worth two in the bush.

Forgery (p. 111)
hotel (1677); sweetling (1648); luncheon (1652); inebrious (1837); the necess'ry (1772); meet his maker (1933); ugly weather (1744)

Works cited

Aldus, Vicky and Morven Dooner (eds). 2008. *Chambers Gigglossary: A Lexicon of Laughter.* Chambers Harrap.

Anglesey Writers Group. 2013. *Môntage: Writings from a Welsh Island.* Bridge Books.

Bhalla, Jag. 2009. *I'm Not Hanging Noodles on Your Ears and Other Intriguing Idioms from Around the World.* National Geographic.

Bierce, Ambrose. 1906/1996. *The Devil's Dictionary.* Wordsworth Reference.

Bombaugh, C C. 1871. *Gleanings for the Curious.* Worthington, Connecticut.

Branford, Jean and Michael Venter. 2016. *Say Again?: The Other Side of South African English.* Pharos Dictionaries.

Crystal, David. 2006. *As They Say in Zanzibar.* HarperCollins.

Crystal, David. 2007. *By Hook or by Crook.* HarperCollins.

Crystal, David. 2015. *The Disappearing Dictionary: A Treasury of Lost English Dialect Words.* Macmillan.

Crystal, David. 2016. *The Unbelievable Hamlet Discovery.* Crystal Books.

Crystal, David. 2017. *The Story of Be.* Oxford University Press.

Crystal, David and Ben Crystal. 2015. *You Say Potato: A Book about Accents.* Pan Macmillan.

Eckler, Ross. 1996. *Making the Alphabet Dance: Recreational Wordplay.* St. Martin's Press.

Espy, Willard R. 1971. *The Game of Words.* Readers Union Group.

Espy, Willard R. 1975. *An Almanac of Words at Play.* Clarkson N Potter.

Ferris, Paul (ed.). 1985. *Dylan Thomas: The Collected Letters.* Macmillan.

Kleiser, Grenville. 1910. *Phrases for Public Speakers.* Funk & Wagnall.

Lederer, Richard. 2023. *A Feast of Words*. Waterside Productions.
Leigh, Percival. 1840/1989. *The Comic English Grammar*. Bracken Books.
Marquis, Don. 1998. *the archy and mehitabel omnibus*. Faber & Faber.
McKean, Erin. 2001. *Verbatim: From the Bawdy to the Sublime, the Best Writing on Language for Word Lovers, Grammar Mavens, and Armchair Linguists*. Harvest Books.
Mieder, Wolfgang and Stewart A Kingsbury (eds). 1994. *A Dictionary of Wellerisms*, Oxford University Press.
Opie, Iona and Peter Opie. 1959. *The Lore and Language of Schoolchildren*. Oxford University Press.
Orton, Harold, Stewart Sanderson and John Widdowson. 1978. *The Linguistic Atlas of England*. Croom Helm.
Partridge, Eric. 1961. *Comic Alphabets: Their Origin, Development, Nature*. Routledge & Kegan Paul.
Partridge, Eric. 1963. *The Gentle Art of Lexicography*. Andre Deutsch.
Partridge, Eric (ed.). 1963. *Swift's Polite Conversation*. Andre Deutsch.
Pickles, Wilfred. 1949. *Between You and Me*. Werner Laurie.
Share, Bernard. 1997. *Slanguage – a Dictionary of Irish Slang and Colloquial English in Ireland*. Gill & Macmillan.
Skeat, Walter. 1910. *Early English Proverbs*. Clarendon Press.
Smith, Linell and Isabel Eberstadt. 1983. *Candy is Dandy: The Best of Ogden Nash*. Mandarin Humour Classics.
Wilkes, G A. 1978. *A Dictionary of Australian Colloquialisms*. Sydney University Press.
Winer, Lise. 2009. *Dictionary of the English Creole of Trinidad & Tobago*. McGill-Queen's University Press.
Wright, Ernest Vincent. 1939/2004. *Gadsby*. Ramble House.
Wright, Joseph. 1906. *English Dialect Dictionary*. University of Innsbruck: https://eddonline-proj.uibk.ac.at
Zettersten, Arne. 1969. *The English of Tristan da Cunha*. Lund Studies in English 37. Gleerup.

Acknowledgements

The author would like to acknowledge the following sources of quoted matter within the text.

P. 45: Lindon, J. A. "Palindromic and Acrostic Poems." *Word Ways* 4, no. 4 (1971): 45. https://digitalcommons.butler.edu/wordways/vol4/iss4/17.

P. 98–99: Nash, Ogden, "How now, sirrah? Oh, anyhow", "England Expects", "Nature Knows Best", "No Wonder Our Fathers Died" and "Where There's a Will, There's Velleity", in *I'm a Stranger Here Myself* (New York: Simon & Schuster, 1938).

Nash, Ogden, "Ode to the N.W. by W. Wind", in *The Primrose Path* (New York: Simon & Schuster, 1936).

P. 57: Dylan Thomas, "Letter to Pamela Hansford Johnson, 21 December 1933", in *The Collected Letters of Dylan Thomas*, ed. Paul Ferris (London: J.M. Dent, 1985).

Index

RAISING READERS

Books Build Bright Futures

Dear Reader,

We'd love your attention for one more page to tell you about the crisis in children's reading, and what we can all do.

Studies have shown that reading for fun is the **single biggest predictor of a child's future life chances** – more than family circumstance, parents' educational background or income. It improves academic results, mental health, wealth, communication skills, ambition and happiness.[1]

The number of children reading for fun is in rapid decline. Young people have a lot of competition for their time. In 2024, 1 in 10 children and young people in the UK aged 5 to 18 did not own a single book at home.[2]

Hachette works extensively with schools, libraries and literacy charities, but here are some ways we can all raise more readers:

- Reading to children for just 10 minutes a day makes a difference
- Don't give up if children aren't regular readers – there will be books for them!
- Visit bookshops and libraries to get recommendations
- Encourage them to listen to audiobooks
- Support school libraries
- Give books as gifts

There's a lot more information about how to encourage children to read on our website: **www.RaisingReaders.co.uk**

Thank you for reading.

hachette UK

[1] OECD, '21st-Century Readers: Developing Literacy Skills in a Digital World', 2021, https://www.oecd.org/en/publications/21st-century-readers_a83d84cb-en.html

[2] National Literacy Trust, 'Book Ownership in 2024', November 2024, https://literacytrust.org.uk/research-services/research-reports/book-ownership-in-2024